Ultimate Voiceover

Getting started, getting hired and getting better!

JEFF LUPETIN

Edited by Joe Wallace

ISBN: 1492888184
ISBN 13: 9781492888185
Library of Congress Control Number: 2013919903
CreateSpace Independent Publishing Platform
North Charleston, South Carolina

INTRODUCTION:

What do you look for when choosing a voice-over teacher/coach? That's an important question because the Internet has allowed far too many un-qualified "teachers" anxious to take your money and run - to flourish. The "Turn-Key" programs, The "Master Classes" and "Killer Demos" all guaranteed to jump-start your career and reap a huge return on your investment sound-and are- too good to be true.

But with this book you've found a working voice over pro willing to share the knowledge and skills that only 30 plus years of professional experience actually DOING voiceovers provides. Here is a straightforward, honest and extremely detailed picture of the voice-over industry *today* and what it takes to compete *today,* skillfully and enthusiastically presented. No nonsense, no promises, other than it will take time and hard work to learn the craft and become "bookable."

This book is a pleasure to read and I've had the pleasure of working and hiring the author many times over the years. I admire his talent, his candor, his teaching and now his writing - immeasurably.

SFX: Drumroll.

"Ladies & Gentlemen your guide, mentor and coach: Jeff Lupetin!"

Harlan Hogan
2014

DEDICATION

This book is dedicated to all my students who had the trust to hire me as their voiceover teacher, coach, or demo producer. It has been great meeting you all and greater helping you begin and enhance your careers.

I would like to thank all the talented advertising writers, producers, and directors who hired me over three decades so that I could excel as a voiceover actor. All the knowledge I gained in the thousands of voice sessions is present in this book.

I would like to thank the following people who were instrumental to my growing my teaching business:

First, Patricia Battaglia, who enlisted me to teach my first voiceover seminar at the Noyes Cultural Art Center in Evanston that began this whole journey. Thanks, Patti!

Julie Cohen, who gave up her beginner class at the Audition Studio in Chicago so I could begin teaching.

Kurt Naebig, who let me replace her.

Actor extraordinaire, Chris Agos, who shared info on his own fine book, "Acting in Chicago".

Rachael Patterson, my current boss, who is great to work for, at Acting Studio Chicago.

Professor Barbara Calabrese, Mary Mattucci Marssie Mencotti and Tom Joyce for helping me to create a Voice for Animation class at Columbia College.

The folks at BAM Studios, including owner Brian Reed and my demo partner, David Leffel, for a great professional environment for our voiceover demo production business.

My editor, Joe Wallace, who showed great enthusiasm right from the beginning. His careful review and outlook helped shape the information in this book.

My son Zach and daughter Lila who each Christmas had a personal wish for me to complete this book.

My wife Betsy Lupetin whose excitement for the book and all its possibilities has been a guiding light. And finally my mother-in-law Tobie Fink, who kept asking me, “Did you finish your book yet?”

Well, I finally got there.

Thanks for all my readers present and future. I hope you learn a lot from this book and have a great career.

Now...Let’s begin and learn a thing or two.

PART I
Getting Started!

"They say I have a great voice for voiceovers."

Introduction

You may have a great voice for voiceovers, but just like hitting a nail doesn't make you a carpenter, having a good voice doesn't make you a voiceover actor. It is a craft, and there are many separate skills sets to learn. Having a voice that sounds good doesn't hurt, but there is much more to it than that. That is why I have written *Ultimate Voiceover,* to give you the inside track on how to approach this business the right way and develop practices and habits that will increase your opportunity for success.

Almost thirty years ago, I began my voiceover career. At the time, I had the ability, the drive, and a great agent, but these alone were not enough for me to succeed. I had to figure out, on the run, the essential components of the business such as how to give a great audition, how to perform under the pressure of a recording session, how to handle rejection, how to market myself, and much more. It wasn't easy, but after years of trial and error, I developed as a talent and became highly successful in a very competitive field.

As a newcomer, I walked into auditions and saw the heavy hitters, some making up to a million dollars a year. It was very daunting. But being a pugnacious sort, I was determined to make my mark.

At first, I approached the audition like a tennis match or basketball game and was highly aggressive and competitive. I was out to beat my opponent each time. This approach failed miserably. My first agent, Pam Jefferson, often told me to calm down because I was too intense at the audition. I thought the copywriters and producers were trying to keep work from me and that I had to snatch it back. I saw other talent—agency favorites—and felt even more behind the eight ball. So many times I would ask Pam "Who got the spot?" and the answer would be "Larry." It drove me crazy. Larry had the in and the ability to deliver. I had talent but was way too hard on myself. I really did not like auditioning and being judged for work when I felt I could do the job easily. I had an attitude. I was just not at all comfortable with the process.

I graded myself on the back of each failed audition script, partly for presentation and partly for the choices I had made. I can still see myself crossing over the Chicago River muttering to myself, "Jeez, what does it take to make it in this business?"

Partly it was learning how talent like Larry did it. I listened to his demo and others, like my friend Joel Cory. I watched how they marketed their talent and dealt with the clients. I listened to their sounds and did my best to present something similar but in my own style. Then the biggest change came.

After failing again and again, particularly at Leo Burnett—the plum agency at the time—I took a different approach. I started reading some self-help books about the power of our thoughts. I read *The Power of your Subconscious Mind* by Dr. Joseph Murphy. It spoke of thinking positive thoughts and wishing others well to create good in your life. These were totally foreign concepts to me.

Day by day I improved my life by applying the tools Dr. Murphy had laid out. After a while, I progressed from an aggressive athletic modality to a creative cooperative modality. Soon I felt I had something to offer: a service that would make companies' spots great. I wanted to give them something, not take something. This relaxed me, and my attitude and success rate changed dramatically. I became easy and fun to work with, and my natural talents flowed out. Knowing that I wanted to give them my talent and to be of service tapped into the better part of my nature—the part that was perfect for the voiceover business. This book and others like it became my personal guides to keeping my thoughts about the business positive.

Thanks to the great agents, voiceover actors, recording-studio engineers, and creative talents at advertising agencies I've had the pleasure to work with, I gained valuable insight about the voiceover business and learned a lot about myself as well. Now I want to pass that knowledge along to you!

Outside of the techniques I will teach you, voice immersion is a huge factor in achieving success in the voiceover business. Like many of my compadres in the VO business, I wanted to do crazy character voices.

Being a baby boomer, television was my unofficial training ground. My inspirations were the great Mel Blanc and Daws Butler, who provided colorful and crazy voices on Warner Brothers and Hanna-Barbera cartoons. Bugs Bunny, Daffy Duck, Foghorn Leghorn, Huckleberry Hound, Snagglepuss, and more gave me fertile sounds to play with and then imitate. How about Jay Ward and June Foray with Rocky and Bullwinkle? And let's not forget Popeye and all the Disney characters. As a kid, I watched and listened and then manipulated my voice to imitate what I heard—interactive television in its infancy. I must also pay tribute to the funny hosts of kid shows, like the great Soupy Sales and his zany cast of characters, including White Fang, Black Tooth, and Pookie. They made me laugh, so I copied their voices so they could make me laugh forever.

In addition, I took great pleasure in crafting impersonations of famous television and film personalities. I was lucky to witness the greatest entertainers of the twentieth century, from Bob Hope and Bing Crosby to Louis Armstrong and Nat King Cole—not to mention the great comedians Johnny Carson and Jonathon Winters and sportscasters like Mel Allen, Marv Albert, and Howard Cosell. There were so many voices and so much to learn. I remember seeing *The Godfather* in New York City with my family. On the ride home, I crafted my best Don Corleone voice, one that I have been hired multiple times to record. Nobody was paying me back then—it was just fun. It still is.

My official voice training started in college. I graduated with a degree in Radio, TV, and Film from Northwestern University. My talents were honed doing the improvisational-comedy review and *The Mee-Ow Show* and while working at the school's radio station, WNUR. I never took an acting class and still do not have any professional acting training. Yet I have learned a lot about acting from doing commercials. All those cold script reads trained me while I wasn't looking.

The majority of my students come from a strong acting background, which helps in this field. However, if you like using and manipulating your voice and have background experience in comedy, improvisation, singing, public speaking or even just sales, this business can work for you as well. Each of these already requires one of the basics of being a good voiceover actor: controlling your voice, being able to express many emotions and thoughts smoothly and easily, and managing words well. It's important to practice delivering voices from different parts of your register. I was doing this as a kid, not aware I was preparing for my profession years in advance.

I was a blue-collar kid; my mom and dad working at the General Motors auto plant in Tarrytown, New York. The idea of doing voices for a living was a foreign concept to everyone in my family. When I first told my relatives I was majoring in TV and film, they wanted me to climb up on their roof fix their TV reception!

I had been out of Northwestern University for eight years when I first got into the VO business. I bumped around in a variety of jobs, mostly on the production side. One day when I was working for a commercial producer—Telemation Productions in Glenview, Illinois—they had me stand in front of the lights to be lit until the talent arrived. I realized in that moment that I wanted to be in front of the camera or mike, not in the shadows. I got back into comedy with the Practical Theatre Company. They offered me a spot in *Megafun*, which ran six months to critical success at the Second City ETC Theater in Chicago. From there I got an agent and a job doing children's programming at WFLD TV 32 and later at WGBO Grant Broadcasting in Chicago. My career was launched.

It must be said here that once I decided to become talent, everything happened in rapid fashion. But as I have pointed out, I had a lot to learn. I was cocky about my voice talent but had to learn to refine it for broadcast. It took me a while to get used to auditioning since I had no acting background to fall back on.

Just before this time, I had worked very hard to be an advertising copywriter. I met with countless ad people, and they encouraged me to do voiceover. I had recordings of some spots I had done with my old comedy troupe Laughtrack. Going up and down those elevators to present my ad work paid dividends later when I returned as a fledgling voiceover talent. I knew the secretaries and the location of each agency, so I was more comfortable being there. Plus, the ad people welcomed me to audition for their spots. I call this the Geography of the Business: knowing where things are so you are comfortable in your surroundings. This applies to studios, too. The more times you enter a great studio like BAM Studios, CRC, Another Country or ARU in Chicago, the more relaxed you will be in your work.

As my commercials began to appear on national television, my dad and my mom became my greatest fans, excited to hear "Jeffrey's voice" coming out of their television set. My dad would brag about me as he heard me in relatives' houses across my hometown of Ossining, New York.

Since then my voice has been heard on TV, radio, slot machines, and pinball machines as well as video games (Gillian Seed from *Snatcher*) and movie theaters. It's even been heard on *Oprah*. **Check out my website at Ultimatevoiceover.com and take a drive through my career.**

Much has changed since the beginning of my career. The major networks still exist, but the work has splintered significantly as cable and the internet have become a larger and cheaper ways to advertise. My competition then was AFTRA and SAG union talent. Non-union talent existed but was silently relegated to the backwaters of the business. Celebrities were making initial inroads, but there were still many plum jobs for us locals.

Now the competition is heavy from above and below. Since the major union-led 6 six-month strike of 2000, we have seen television change with the advent of reality television. Sitcoms and dramatic series that housed hundreds of actors were eliminated, so actors needed to make money elsewhere. The celebrity crowd moved to commercials, and their presence is now immense. More and more producers and writers seek celebrities to do their work, even if they are only heard and not seen. It sounds crazy, but it's true. Today's voiceover environment has become one big Walmart, with producers seeking cheaper talent from the non-union sector. As the economy shifts and budgets tighten, advertising creative teams move to eliminate residual payments (pay after your initial session costs) for non-union talent. You can still be cast as a Union actor, but it is much more difficult that when I began my career in 1983.

On top of that, you no longer meet your creative team at the agency level. You audition at your agent's office or from home with little or no direction. You don't develop a relationship with the ad people like you did before. You are more on your own. Commercials, if they run on the networks, run for shorter periods of time. You can't count on that income as you once did. Many agencies buy time here and there, not investing primarily in the traditional TV and radio commercial format.

Today, with the advertising industry raking in over $12 billion in revenue, there certainly is a lot of voiceover work going on. But where is it? And how do you get connected to it to create a stream of income in this field? You will learn to mine your connections, getting inside tracks to work that can be your own private island. The client may love your voice and use you consistently on their voiceover projects. Other times, you will be cast, used once, and then never again. It's all good! Your job will be simple: audition well, market well, and do good work. You can get caught up in all kinds of tricky thoughts, but keep it simple. Work your connections, prepare for and do good auditions, and then be a professional in the studio so they will want you back again.

When I began my career, I saw tons of opportunity ahead. I knew I could do VO at a high level because I had been playing around with voices since I was young. However, it took much more than being the man of a thousand voices to succeed.

One of my first jobs was playing Dracula with my friend and fellow funny voice artist Marie Burke. Later I played Bogart to Peter Lorre in a *Casablanca*-style spot with an established male actor. I was quiet in those days, just showing up and looking over my script. In this case, the other actor thought I was an ad guy and started to openly audition for my role, doing random Bogart dialogue to impress the creative team in the studio. As I slowly put my script on the copy stand, his eyes widened and sheepishly asked me if I was talent. I smiled and said,

"Yes, I am playing the Bogart role."

He apologized and we became friendly after that. This is just some of the stuff that can happen in a session.

Character voices and impressions were fun to do, but to survive I had to widen my repertoire. I had to learn to be myself on the mike—to just talk naturally like I did in life. Oddly enough, I found this a difficult task.

I was taken on for a national TV spot and muffed it because I simply could not be myself. The more I tried, the worse it got. They kept saying, "Just be yourself," and I kept saying to myself, "What the hell is that?"

I was replaced and watched the dollar signs melt before my eyes. I still can feel the helplessness of not knowing what to do in that situation. I know the solution now and can pass it along to you so you'll never have to go through that kind of disappointment. That is what *Ultimate Voiceover* is all about: learning techniques that will keep you out of the potholes of this business.

Mind-set is key in this business. You audition a lot and most times with no tangible results. No matter how successful you are, it is easy to get down on yourself and your talents. When that happens, you press, try too hard, and really muck up your work. I have always said you need a" Give a damn but not give a damn attitude." You should care about doing a great read but still act free and easy like your life doesn't depend on it. This is something you will learn over time. I hit my head on the wrong door many times and eventually had no other door to enter but the right one. Remember, as my friend David Lewis from VOX Casting always tells disheartened voice actors, it is your job to match the voice in the writer's head. Sometimes you do and sometimes, no matter how great the audition, it is not you they are hearing. Try not to take it so personally.

Also, be good to your fellow voice actors. Wish them well, and good things will come to you, too. This new knowledge came to me from impregnating my mind with new thoughts and replacing the ones that did me harm. Dr. Murphy's book and others worked wonders and allowed me to imagine my success and put positive energy into achieving it. Many of the works of Catherine Ponder also reflect this basic theory: change your thoughts to change your life. I still need to reread these works from time to time to keep myself from sliding back into entitled behavior.

Many of these books almost popped off the shelf as I looked for more to read. They made me feel there was more than just dumb luck to being successful. If not for these readings and the hard work I did day in and day out to apply these principles, I am convinced I would not have succeeded as I did.

This simple shift in attitude helped me enjoy the business and my fellow voice actors. We all want to win the spot, but I found that the business was best when more of us were working, supporting our families, and making great money using the sounds of our own voices. Almost thirty years later, I still feel the same way. There is no greater birthday present than to stand in front of a microphone and record a commercial. It is still fun and feels so good.

Okay. Lets talk about you and your future career in voiceover. Whether you are a beginner with no experience, a voice actor who has done a few spots, or an experienced pro, there is something in *Ultimate Voiceover* for you.

I am writing this book to fast-forward *your* success, sharing all that I learned so you can progress quickly in your career. For the beginner, I will build the infrastructure for you to *audition well* and *record well.* I will cover the technical and mental aspects of learning the business. You will discover what it takes to get into voice acting and succeed as a voice actor. For the established actor, I will share techniques that can *improve your auditions.* I will present insights that will keep you zoned in and give you an authentic read, making you *a bigger player in the business.*

My goals for you are to be able to do the following:

- Walk into each audition and recording session as a professional.
- Take charge in marking up your script and making it yours.
- Fully engage in the creative process of doing a commercial, taking direction and making corrections on the fly that will get the job done.
- Handle the psychological part of this business.
- Market yourself.
- Deal with the financial aspects of the voiceover business.

You can do it! It just takes application of the techniques I am offering and your consistent ability to apply them. Like in sports, practice right and play right. There is a lot of information in this book. Apply it piece by piece and go over it again and again. Don't just gulp it down. Let it guide you throughout your career. Keep this book as a valuable resource along your journey.

I have taught voiceover in classes and individually to people just like you. Taking the time to read this book and apply my techniques means you're already on the way to getting where you ultimately need to be in the voiceover business. Thanks for reading *Ultimate Voiceover*, and I look forward to hearing from you about how my techniques help you along the way.

Why shouldn't *you* be the next success story?

Sections:

Let's begin with some basics.

So What the Heck Is Voiceover Anyway?

Voiceover is the usage of the voice only to sell a product or service or to help tell a story. Simply, you are heard and never seen in a voiceover. Radio commercials consist entirely of voiceover. The unseen announcers on television spots are all voice actors, too. They tell you to buy that flashy Mercedes, to fly American Airlines to Florida, or to hurry into McDonald's for the new value meals. Voiceovers can be heard as narrators on the History Channel who tell the story of a great Civil War battle or exploration into space. An actor playing the voice of an animated character for cartoons or for video game characters is also doing a voiceover.

Voice actors talk over the visual—the actors or action on-screen. Hence the name *voiceover*: the voice goes over the action. Here is a list of the most common types of voiceovers:

- Radio commercials.
- Television commercials.
- Promos for television stations (e.g., "Next on Fox...").
- Narrations (e.g., History Channel Civil War documentaries).
- Movie Trailers: trailers
- Movie voiceover narration.
- Pinball game voices.
- Video game voices.
- Slot machine voices.
- Corporate training videos and films.
- Animated film, video, and cartoon voices.
- Phone prompts (e.g., "Thanks for calling Remcore...").
- Prerecorded messages (e.g., "And now, ladies and gentlemen...").

Again, the actual human talking is heard and not seen. Voiceovers can be heard in movies, too. In the film *Raising Arizona*, actor Nicholas Cage is heard but not seen while telling his story at the beginning and end of the film. The same is true of Morgan Freeman in *Million Dollar Baby*. He speaks over the action on the screen.

Anatomy of a Successful VO Actor

In my judgment, a successful voiceover actor has the following traits:

- **Good vocal tone.** Has a voice that cuts through and a strong, sexy, clean, deep, interesting, funny, clear, or soothing vocal tone. Enjoyable to hear a story told by him or her.

- **Good reader.** Knows how to read copy smoothly, easily, and in time. Manages copy well. Improves read through multiple takes. Can compress breath for quicker reads.
- **Good breath control.** Can hold the note, sound, and tone of the read. Can hold the intensity of the information piece of the script. Prior singing experience is helpful.
- **Good actor.** Translates the tone of each script and tells the story in a believable way. For character work, offers different choices and voices. Good at improvisation.
- **Good personality.** Easy to work with and a fun person to be around. Has a pleasant professional attitude and is easy to hire again and again. After all, who do you like to hang out with: someone fun or someone who's a pain in the neck?
- **Good flexibility.** Takes direction well. Has ability to shift and offer different choices in a script.
- **Good marketing skills.** Can put out a demo and promotional pieces such as a website that sells his or her own name as well as the client's.
- **Perseverance.** Doesn't give up. Sets goals and achieves them. Pushes talent to the limit. Rolls with the punches and handles the ups and downs of the business. Is a self-motivator who doesn't wait for the agent to do it all for him or her.
- **Good intuition.** Can match the voice in the client's head for the spot. Makes subtle changes before being directed to do so.

Of course, there are always exceptions to the rules here. But based on my years of experience in the business, the consensus seems to be that these are the best qualities a voice actor could have.

Celebrity voiceover talent may get a bit more leeway in some of these areas due to his or her built-in name recognition. Some behaviors may not match what I have outlined here, but overall, one should cultivate these qualities to ensure a long career in the voiceover business.

Again, remember that voiceover actors are actors who can control and use their voices with expertise in front of a microphone. Just because you are a fine stage actor doesn't mean you can transition easily into being a great voiceover actor. On stage, you project your voice—you supply the volume so the audience can hear you. In voiceovers, the microphone does the work for you, so a quieter, more focused, more conversational voice is needed.

You may have some or all of these qualities. Do an inventory on yourself and see where your strengths and weaknesses lie. You can always improve in any of these categories. I am raising the bar high for you to show you the full picture of how great you can be, but it is important to have reasonable expectations when taking on this business.

The Roads to Voiceover

First...

Students and Inspired Novices

Johnny or Judy sure talks a lot. Maybe we could use all that chatter and put it to good use to get that college fund jump-started. Not a bad idea, Mom and Dad. However, if you wanted your child to make money on the tennis circuit, I think there might be some training involved. The same is true here. Training in improvisation, acting, and singing sure would help a fledgling young voiceover take shape. Most importantly in this whole process, does your son or daughter like to use his or her voice for fun? Is it a form of play?

ULTIMATE VOICEOVER TIP!

If you love playing with your voice for free, this may be the business for you!

Ah, yes. There I am: young Jeff Lupetin parked in front of a television set soaking up cartoons and whatever else is being broadcast between test pattern sign-ons and sign-offs. I start imitating what I hear, and a career begins. Did I know that then? No way. But I had fun with voices and recorded myself later for free and enjoyed it. So the litmus test is this: Is it fun for you and would you record for free and still love it? If the answer is yes, you, my friend, could be a budding VO artist.

So let's assume you've always wanted to do funny voices or maybe any kind of voice at all and get paid for it. It sure seems like fun. It is, like getting the victory parade down Main Street, but getting there is work. If you are willing to put in the time, energy, and money to train yourself and then go out auditioning, the road could lead to success. There are no guarantees here—just things that tend to lead to success. You don't have to be great—just persistent in training and connecting with clients. And you have to love to get in front of a microphone in a studio and talk.

If you are open to learning and getting better and better, hey, get out of the way—here you come.

Prospective voiceover talent come from a variety of initial professions or jobs before taking the plunge into the wild world of voiceover acting. Some voice actors continue in their other jobs part-time to keep money flowing in as they get established. I would recommend this while you ease into this profession. Having another steady stream of income will keep the pressure off of your fledgling VO career bearing lots of fruit financially at first.

Here are some common professions or jobs that work best while beginning voiceover work.

Acting

This is a no-brainer. Being trained as an actor helps you to interpret copy at a high level.
Also, as an actor you may already have an agent who can help you segue into the voiceover business. Performing in a play or movie is a great shortcut to meeting people who are enamored with your talents and would like you to work for them on some commercials.

It's great to have some heat around you as a performer to get started in the VO business.
Acting prepares you to think on your feet and shift from style to style.

Radio or Television Broadcasting

Radio and television personalities have an easier entry into VO in that they are known commodities in many cases and have the skill set to compete at a high level. They are already using their voices every day and know how to get copy across. The only downside can be a sameness to the reads or burn in from reading the news with the exact same cadence each time. This habitual reading is hard to break out of completely unless you are working with a competent and experienced VO coach like...well...me. Whether you are the local weatherperson or doing sports nationally, doing voiceover work is a natural parallel move in the profession. Many times the work is done side by side at the station at which one works. I was a booth announcer for two television stations where I wrote and performed my material.

Jingle Singer or Singing Talent

Lots of voiceover actors once did or continue to do jingle singing as well. Even though the jingle business has diminished over the years, being a singer helps you with breath control, which is vital for reading copy and doing voiceover work. I find that those who have singing experience already know how to add emotion to scripts and get through lengthy copy quickly and easily. Once you can get through copy more easily, you can add more of your personality to the delivery.

Sales

People who come from a sales career have ready advantages that can be used in the business side of voice acting. Sales professionals are adept at building connections to get and maintain a flow of work. Collecting clients is the first step in keeping your career afloat in the voiceover business. Many times sales professionals can reconnect with former clients to seek out corporate voiceover work in, for example, sales films or company presentations.

In addition, sales professionals are used to cold calling and dealing with the rejection inherent in the VO business.

Public Speaking

Those involved with public speaking know how to stand in front of strangers and get their point across with the right emphasis. They know how to break down copy to best communicate key sales points. It has been said that speaking in front of an audience is the next-closest thing to death. It can be very intimidating. Auditioning or recording in front of strangers from the ad world can get you going, too. This is why I ask you to make things stupidly easy in sessions by going slow and breaking down copy to the easiest increments so you have control of your ship. As in public speaking, slowing it down can help immensely. Nerves are OK—just take it slow and easy.

Improvisers

I am biased here in that this was the world I came from to compete in the voiceover arena. I had little acting experience, having been trained in production at Northwestern University. What I learned in improvisational comedy really helped me make interesting choices for voiceover spots.

Changing from voice to voice or character to character was natural for me. Once I got in front of the microphone, I couldn't wait to try out different sounds to create an interesting character for a commercial or video game. My training at NU, Second City, and Piven Theatre Workshop and my experience in comedy clubs really paid dividends. However, when you are in a studio facing strangers, you can clam up and have trouble doing your best. Your nerves can get the best of you.

When I auditioned to be the children's programming voice for WFLD-TV in Chicago, they wanted me to imitate the guy on the air. I hated being like him, but I tried to do it because there was real money on the line. Finally my boss Jon Findley said, "Just turn on the mike and do your characters. Don't hold back or edit." What I did then is what became my on-air persona and the voices I used for all the promos in the morning and afternoon lineups. I just let it rip, using my improvisational training to create on the spot. It was fun stuff.

In a session, you may have certain standby voices, but the writers may ask, "What else to do you have?" At this point you have to throw something at the microphone.

ULTIMATE VOICEOVER TIP!

When auditioning character voices, learn to throw something at the mike.

You have your old standbys: voices that have been cast before. When the writer or producer asks what else you have, make a sound, support it with breath, talk through it and throw it at the mike; you may not know where it is going, but talk through it and let it land.

This can feel really scary because you are afraid of looking bad; however, the gold lies here in on-the-spot creation. Don't worry about whether the voice will land or fall apart. Just move on to the next one. Trust that your voice will not stay with a sound that just can't be supported.

So what if none of these professions, jobs, or skills are in your background?

Do not despair. As you will see in the next section, you can still get started right away and lay the groundwork for your success. It will take hard work, a large time investment, talent, and money to move forward. But if you do—and if you like the process—there could be a place for you in the business.

Who Hires Voiceover Talent?

Voiceover talent is hired in the following ways for these different types of jobs:

- **TV and radio commercials.** Hired by advertising creatives assigned to the account you are voicing for.
    - **Example.** FCB Chicago handles SC Johnson products. You audition to be the announcer for Off! bug spray at home or from your agent's recording space. The ad team assigned to your commercials will select the talent.
- **Non-broadcast corporate.** Hired by audio engineers or audio creatives at the specific company your work is for.
    - **Example.** McDonald's corporate is looking to do a training video. Jim Smith is head of audio at McDonald's corporate. He sends the audition to the agents. They select who they believe to be appropriate to audition and send the auditions to Jim to decide.
- **Television and radio station in-house commercials.** Hired by TV and radio stations as full-time employees (booth announcers do all station promos and ads). These commercials are done daily by a salaried employee. You don't audition for this work.
- **Promo announcing.** Hired by show producers or Station Managers for creative daily voice work

    Example. *The Oprah Winfrey Show* is looking for an announcer for a special show on the 1960s. They contact a recording studio or agents and ask for talent auditions. The talent is sent to the *Oprah* creative team who decide who they want for this one program.

Example. Ellen is looking for a new promo announcer for her show. They send the script to talent agents who select talent to read. The auditions are sent to Ellen DeGeneres's production people, and they decide.

- **Movie promos.** Hired by studios producing films. This is perhaps the most difficult voicing area to crack. Don La Fontaine regaled us for years with his "in a world" style of announcing. Agents can submit for movie promos, but the opportunities are for a select few at this time.

- **Audio books.** These gigs can come through your agent, but they come mostly from various companies, many centered in NY. There are a few in the Midwest as well. They require days of reading and a lot of preparation before recording.

- **Internet website announcer.** Hired by local company in charge of audio projects. The boss might be in charge of this, or it might be someone he assigns the task.

- **Local car dealer ads.** Hired by an ad agency assigned to the dealer or by the dealer himself in smaller markets. In most cases, an advertising or public relations company will be involved in the hiring. Your voiceover agent will handle the audition and submit for you.

Online Sites

You can also be hired through Internet casting services like Voices.com, Voice123, and Voicebank.net. Individual companies will post scripts, and you can be selected by the company creative team handling the product. These can be projects of all shapes and sizes. You also may be required to record from your home. This means you are the engineer as well as the VO talent.

The good part of this is that you don't need an agent to get work through these sites; the bad news is you will not be sure how reputable the producers of these spots are. Also you must have suitable equipment to create a professional sound for the voiceover. In addition, it will usually take much longer to get paid, and you may run into more issues than a union talent who has enforced deadlines for payment.

I'm not saying using websites is bad. In fact, it might be a good start. The work, however, can and should get better with training and experience.

How Much Should I Get Paid?

That is a good question. There are also different prices for union and nonunion actors. The union actor has a set price structure for his or her work, while the nonunion actor's session fees can vary from producer to producer.

Here are a few ideas as to how much you should expect for different kinds of voiceover work.

SAG-AFTRA union rates (as of this writing)

A SAG-AFTRA TV spot pays you $445.30
A SAG-AFTRA Radio spot pays you $262.50.

These are considered scale costs, with no extra fees attached.
At times you may get what is called "LA scale " which is scale and a half. It is called LA scale to cover the additional cost of traveling to the spot that are needed in the Los Angeles market.

Your agent in a market such as Chicago or NY might pitch you for that cost, but most times actors will receive a scale payment as listed above.

Residuals rates and other voiceover payments can be accessed by going to SAG-AFTRA web site.

Voice123 Internet Casting: General Rates (Including Overall Rates for Non-broadcasts and Small-Market Broadcasts)

These rates apply to voiceover work that will be used in promos, commercials, documentaries, and shows for radio, TV, cable, and the Internet in small markets. It also covers narrations, audiobooks, podcasts, corporate and industrial presentations, video games, films, movie trailers, multimedia (CD/DVD), websites, phone systems (IVR), on-hold messages, voicemails, and more.

Recordings for broadcasts in regional and large markets tend to have more expensive rates. Please see below.

Radio (Including Internet Radio)

	US Dollars		Euros	
	Median	Average	Median	Average
15 seconds	100	107	120	171
30 seconds	150	158	155	192
60 seconds	200	216	225	252

TV and Cable

	US Dollars		Euros	
	Median	Average	Median	Average
15 seconds	150	167	175	254
30 seconds	200	239	210	240
60 seconds	280	310	285	311

All Others

Per minute of audio delivered:	US Dollars		Euros	
	Median	Average	Median	Average
Up to 2 minutes	100	100	75	75
Up to 5 minutes	75	84	40	42
Up to 10 minutes	50	72	30	30
Up to 20 minutes	42	63	23	26
Up to 60 minutes	30	63	13	14
Each additional minute over 60 minutes	20	45	10	11

Per word:	US Dollars	
	Median	Average
From 100 to 250 words	0.40	0.81
Up to 500 words	0.38	0.54
Up to 1000 words	0.30	0.47
Up to 2000 words	0.24	0.43
Up to 6000 words	0.20	0.34
Each word over 6000 words	0.15	0.20

Per hour of work (regardless of the length of the audio delivered):	US Dollars	
	Median	Average
One hour or less	200	238
Up to 2 hours	170	213
Up to 5 hours	150	183
Up to 10 hours	130	164
Up to 20 hours	120	153
Up to 60 hours	100	143
Each hour over 60 hours	100	134

Rates for Regional Market Broadcasts

These rates apply to voiceover work that will be used in promos, commercials, documentaries, and shows for radio, TV, cable, and the Internet in *regional* markets:

Radio (Including Internet Radio)

	US Dollars	
	Median	Average
15 seconds	105	145
30 seconds	170	208
60 seconds	200	274

TV and Cable

	US Dollars	
	Median	Average
15 seconds	200	219
30 seconds	250	301
60 seconds	350	399

All Others

Per minute of audio delivered	US Dollars	
	Median	Average
Up to 2 minutes	85	110
Up to 5 minutes	75	100
Up to 10 minutes	65	91
Up to 20 minutes	58	79
Up to 60 minutes	50	76
Each additional minute over 60 minutes	44	52

These rates apply to voiceover work that will be used in promos, commercials, documentaries, and shows for radio, TV, cable, and the Internet in *large* markets (including national markets and very large metro areas).

Radio (Including Internet Radio)

	US Dollars	
	Median	Average
15 seconds	200	250
30 seconds	250	334
60 seconds	400	452

TV and Cable

	US Dollars	
	Median	Average
15 seconds	275	381
30 seconds	400	492
60 seconds	500	686

All Others

Per minute of audio delivered	US Dollars	
	Median	Average
Up to 2 minutes	100	151
Up to 5 minutes	100	145
Up to 10 minutes	88	126
Up to 20 minutes	80	118
Up to 60 minutes	70	160
Each additional minute over 60 minutes	49	70

Union work will pay the most and have ironclad contracts. This will ensure you get paid on-time. If not, you will receive a late fee. Nonunion payments can be comparable at times, though a buyout is often involved. A buyout means one and done with no future payment for that session completed.
Union contracts can be renewed over months and years. If a contract has run its course, your union agent can bump up the spot by 50 to 100 percent over its old use. That's good money for you.

In non-union situations, rates can be very low or up to union standards. It depends on the producer and his budget. Getting the work is important, but in the long run, I would advise moving to union work if the opportunity is ripe for doing so. This would be the case if you are cast in a union spot and have the opportunity for other such spots. You will know when the time is right. If uncertain, talk with your agent or fellow VO actors and ask them questions. Or e-mail me at Jefflupetin@gmail.com. I will give you my two cents.

Growing Your Voiceover Career

What can you expect when you start out in the voiceover business?

This is a crucial first step when considering your dream of getting business in this field.

What is it like to begin this process? What are reasonable expectations? Just having great talent and a terrific voice is not enough. Perseverance mixed with talent wins the day, in my opinion. How you navigate through the ups and downs will set the tone for your success.

ULTIMATE VOICEOVER TIP!

Take this on as a process.

There is a lot to learn while becoming a professional VO talent. For one, slow and steady wins the race. You don't have to ingest everything whole. Take your time, meet people, enjoy the process, and keep practicing and getting better. It takes time to meet people and learn this business. Enjoy the ride! (End of well-meaning clichés.)

Here are some stages to consider:

Beginning VO talent

- **Learning the business.** Classes, individual coaching, studio or related voice experience, and voice immersion in preparation for seeking an agent for representation. You will be trained to use your voice and find your voice's niche. You should experiment in class with announcers, characters, and narration styles. At the same time, you should be online listening to demos of your accomplished VO actors and paying attention to radio and television spots for voices you can master.

    Potential pitfalls. There will be actors who are way better than you. You may get discouraged and wonder how you can do this—but you can. Keep going and get your training and practice in. Get your individual result.

- **Early sessions.** To get started, you may be doing a few free sessions to get experience. There is nothing wrong with this at first.

Getting time in front of a microphone is always valuable. Make sure you get a copy of the work you have to do for a demo compilation. If you can, ask for fifty to a hundred dollars. Doing favors can get your name around and get you real work in the future. Just don't make a habit of it.

- **Home recording.** Purchasing equipment (a microphone, software, etc.) for practice and future auditions and learning the proper way to record and send in MP3s.

  Potential pitfalls. You may have issues with setting up and using equipment. Seek others who are savvy. They are out there and willing to help. Keep them as reliable sources of help with other issues as they crop up. Let this be a learning curve. Some move quickly; others are lost for a bit. Either way, you will get there and feel good about it.

- **Voiceover demo production.** Finding the right producer for your talents (hint, hint). Creating a professional demo and presenting it to VO agents. Posting the demo on your personal website and Internet VO sites. Presenting the demo to prospective employers.

  Potential pitfalls. You could get lowballed or get lured into accepting super- highly priced price demo production scenarios. Check around and make sure the producer is fair and doesn't offer you the moon.

  Find other actors who are happy with their results. Too low... If it's too low or too high, you will have to record again...too high..., and the result may be that you are out out of funds for the rest of your needs..

Set aside $3000 or so to get yourself started. More will be necessary, but that amount will suffice for classes, individual instruction, recording equipment, and (potentially) a commercial demo reel.

You will need to have a full-time or part-time job while training, and you will have to fit in classes at night or when you have free time during the day. Begin to dream of VO creating new income and the possibility that you will change professions.

Your expected income at this skill level is $2,500 to $10,000.

Intermediate VO Talent

- **Agency representation.** You now have an agent. You send in auditions from home as well as audition at the VO agent's studio.

- **Voiceover auditions.** You will have one or two of these a week.

- **Voiceover sessions.** Being hired for radio, television, and non-broadcast opportunities. You will have one or two of these sessions a month—more if there are redos or they like your voice for their campaign. You may work for one client monthly for different recordings, but usually you will get one spot here and there. It's hard to predict. You may still do a freebie every once in a while to get your name out there and fill the favor bank. Remember: get a quality copy of your work!

- **Marketing:**

    - Getting your demo around and sending out promotional materials (pads, pens, etc.) to tell the world you are here and ready to voice.
    - Setting up an individual webpage to house your demos.

  - Creating an attractive graphic to sell your services.
  - Meeting ad agency creative teams and other clients who like your work.
  - Creating an up-to-date contact list.

- **Money management.** Properly handling money made in the business. Setting up a new account to pay for marketing and equipment needs. You may buy a better microphone and portable equipment for recording. Handling the improvement in your lifestyle.

- **Work situation.** Part-time for audition and session availability. May like the combo of work and VO work. May plan on becoming a full-time VO.

Your expected income at this skill level is $10,000 to $25,000.

ULTIMATE VOICEOVER TIP!

Don't quit your day job…yet!

Doing voice work is much better than sitting in a cubicle all day, but if you have a flexible day job, I would suggest you hold on to it until your VO work really becomes consistent. This will lessen financial stress and let you enjoy your fledgling career more. When things get slow VO-wise, it is nice to have something to prop you up a bit. You don't want to press too hard at first.

Advanced VO Talent

- **Auditions.** You will have three to five of these a week.

- **Voice sessions.** You will have at least two or three of these a week. 2 union jobs with the thought of going AFTRA-SAG or perhaps have been in the unions for a while.

- **Work situation.** Perhaps still working part-time but devoting more and more time to the VO business as your primary source of income. If things are going really well, you might take the business on full-time, though I recommend you have other avenues—on camera or in film and theater—to balance out the dry times.

Your expected income at this skill level is $25,000 to $50,000.

There are some potential pitfalls here:

- **Success.** It has many effects on VO talent. You get hot, and then suddenly you can't win an audition. You may get a big head about your success and a feeling of entitlement when work slows down. You may think you've lost it. You haven't. You press—try too hard—and then it gets worse. You may get cranky or angry from the lack of work or a lesser stream of auditions. You may get mad at your agent about the lack of work. Don't!

ULTIMATE VOICEOVER TIP!

Avoid getting mad at your agent.

It is really easy to get mad at your agent, but it can be a deal killer in your relationship. Remember you are one of many talents and your agent hears complaints all day in between tracking down your money and dealing with flighty VO clients. By all means, express...but with a friend or loved one. One blowup can poison the well and prevent you from getting some plum auditions. Beware!

- **Money.** A common pitfall is spending beyond your means. That network spot is not going to run forever. The car, the condo, or the house—make sure it is in your budget. A big commercial or campaign is a blessing but can skew your thinking. Avoid taking on big expenditures that will last when the spot or campaign ends. Save your money and let this rainfall quench your thirst in dryer times.

- **Attitude.** Big ego and entitlement –it can creep in. It's natural. You go from struggling to being successful in a blink sometimes. But this business is humbling. I have seen many actors fall and hit the ground hard. Keep working, improving, and meeting new potential clients. Keep an attitude of gratitude and you will weather the bumps and bruises well and be back on top soon.

Top Pro Voiceover Talent

- **Auditions.** You will have at least five to ten of these a week.

- **Voice sessions.** You will have at least five of these a week. Congratulations! You are much in demand. Your work now appears on national and local commercials on radio and television. Your voice is easy to cast and easily approved by the many clients who want to use your services. Your hard work and practice has really paid off. It's a beautiful thing!

- **Work situation.** You have many spots on the air so you can depend somewhat on an elevated income. By this time, you are counting on VO as the main source of your income. It's still valuable and helpful to have other sources of income to keep the pressure off. On-camera, film, and stage work would balance things out. If you have a small side business, keep it. Commercials can rain down money and then be gone in an instant. Save a good portion of your income to prevent overspending that can get you in trouble. Enjoy the view! It is great to be on top!

Your expected income at this skill level is $50,000 to $100,000, but it can rise far beyond this.

Once you are a valued commodity in this business, it might feel like you have free access to the bank vault. It can get your head spinning. You may make more in ten to twenty hours than others make in a month or more. You may earn in a year way more than your parents. Keep it in perspective. You deserve it because you worked to get there, but keep your eye on your work. Keep practicing and don't think you are a hotshot. You are not. You are just a successful, in-demand VO actor who is developing a solid career. The key word here is *career*. This can't just last a year or so. You want it to build to carry you into a strong career, where, under a union contract, you get your health benefits and pension laid out for future years. It is a blessing, but keep working and changing a bit with the times. Do not get complacent. Keep your eye on the prize, or it will escape and be hard to find again.

ULTIMATE VOICEOVER TIP!
Run your own ship.

The voiceover business is just that: a business. You need to get comfortable with taking action, motivating yourself, and setting goals that can be achieved. Yes, the agent will be a factor in this, but you are responsible for your audition quality, your session work, and other tasks, such as following up and marketing. An agent is often like a mother with lots of kids. She may love you and believe in you, but she only has so much time to give. It will be much healthier if you run your own ship and take full ownership of your journey.

11 Steps to Get Started Now!

Step One: Read Out Loud a Lot

You should work at a radio station or do podcasts for consistent voice use. My first experience in front of a microphone was in the sixth grade, when I did the morning announcements for Ann M. Dorner Middle School in Ossining, New York. Later, in high school and college, I did radio work. With the advent of the Internet, we can now do our own shows on podcasts for all to hear. What this does is it gets the nervousness out and gets you comfortable with just speaking in front of a microphone.

You will learn to land your voice and get good practice that will help you segue into commercial work. At the station, you will have to do commercial reads live, which will give you good training as well. In Chicago, you can work for CRIS Radio, which reads to the blind. You can decide on the content. Many of my students have gotten initial practice doing this type of reading. There is no shortcut to reading well. You need to read out loud a lot to become comfortable and proficient with handling copy.

Step Two: Take a Class in Improvisation

Improvisation trains you to be quick on your feet, to shift voice choices and create easily on the spot. Things can change quickly in a session. Your ability to improvise and move with the demands of the creative team will help you excel in the session and in your career.

Step Three: Take an Acting Class

- **Part of being a good voiceover actor is being a good actor.** A good actor can translate the ad writer's words and make them reach the hearts and minds of the listening audience. It's that human connection that sells the product. Obviously, we don't normally speak the way ad copy is written. So it takes a good actor to speak words with prices and product points and still get the advertisers words across in a realistic way that sells product. *Being comfortable speaking one-on-one in front of a microphone* and in front of strangers in a recording studio is one of the tricks of voiceover. Taking an acting class or two will teach you valuable ways you can speak to the heart of things. Basically, you will relearn how you communicate in your life by breaking down the components of your thoughts and actions. It's a cool process.

- **Take a class in cold reading.** In voiceover auditions, you get the script, mark it up, and go. You don't memorize your lines like in theater auditions. So the more comfortable you are with cold readings, the better. A cold reading just gives you the lay of the land in the script and helps you to locate difficult words and phrases and hard breath areas. After the cold read, you can course correct and do cleaner and cleaner reads with practice.

- **Read storybooks, especially children's books.** All commercials are essentially brief stories. If you get comfortable with storytelling, you will excel in voiceover commercial reads. Children's books may go from narrator voice to character voice. Good. Have fun with this, and you will see a parallel in shifting tones in voiceover copy—the only difference is that it's less visible.

Step Four: Take a Voiceover Class

- **No voiceover experience? Take a beginner class.** If you have some acting experience but no experience in voiceover, start with a beginner class. If you are a working actor, you might want to move on to intermediate level. In the class, you will study different types of scripts and styles of reading them. You will get to read with your other students and hear other vocal styles. You will learn a lot and get comfortable in front of the microphone. Major cities like Chicago, California, and New York will be teeming with classes and instructors. For smaller markets, you may need to travel and study where the best instructors are or look for local college classes or learning centers that teach voiceover. However, it will pay big dividends for you to study with top-notch professionals who have really worked in the business. Also, big-city professionals are likely to come to your area to give seminars. They should cost $200 to $300. Don't overpay.

- **Study with a current professional in a real studio.** A class taught by working voiceover talent is a great place to start. You will be getting news from the front line, not from a history book. Also, *you will get scripts that are currently on the air.* Hopefully your class will be held in an actual studio and before the actual microphones you will be talking into for quality dollars. It gets you pumped up when you hear your voice coming from the best audio equipment money can buy. You will be more at ease when you show up to a top-notch studio to record your voice session.

- **To find great teachers, check local acting schools and seek out fellow actors.** Go online, check local acting newspapers, or call local agents. Find your local acting schools and see what is available, but please, study only with a current working professional. Expect to pay $400 or more for a class lasting eight weeks or so. Trust me: it is money well spent!

- **Treat your engineer like a king.** If the class is taught in an actual recording studio, treat your engineer like a king. He or she hears voiceover actors every day. He can really help you sound and perform better with well-placed comments on your reads. When making a demo, I believe that the work done by a good engineer is one-third of the process; scripts and your performance make up the rest. He or she may cut you a deal when you need to do a demo. Also, top engineers often hold auditions at their studios. Your engineer friend may call you in repeatedly once he or she knows your voice.

Step Five: Record Yourself

- **Record onto your computer, phone, or tablet.** Technology has greatly changed how we can record our voices. I started with a stereo portable cassette recorder. Before that, the rage was reel-to-reel recording for super-high fidelity. Well, today we start with the computer and move on from there.

  A simple USB mike plugged into your laptop or desktop can get your started. I will give more details on recording setups later in this book. Your smartphone should have an audio utility. On an iPhone, you can use voice memos. I recently downloaded a free app called PCM Recorder from Tascam. This app allows you to adjust the volume of your recording, unlike the voice memo app.

  This is the way to go. Recording on your computer, phone, or tablet allows you to make a clean digital recording of your voice for practice sessions and eventually for audition purposes if necessary. You can archive what you record to check your progress, and as you become savvier, you can even put together demo materials from your computer. When you get an agent, you will be able to record your voice for audition purposes, saving the time and energy of driving down to auditions far away from where you live. All in all, it's a great thing to learn.

  See if your computer has some basic recording software. For instance, a Mac will carry a program like Garage Band. If it does, learn it and put it into play. If your computer does not have recording software, you will need to install or download one, such as any of the following:

- Audacity is free, and you can use right away after downloading it. I would suggest trying this out first before seeing if you need to spend money on another program.

- Sound Forge is perhaps the simplest. You can get a demonstration copy off of the Internet to learn it, and later you should pay for the software if it is what you want to use. You can also find this program at retailers like Best Buy. This is the program used by my agency for all their auditions.

- Pro Tools is the choice of audio engineers in many of the finest studios. This software is usually bundled in for free when you purchase an Mbox mixer. It also comes with an audio training system that will teach you the rudiments of this software.

Set up a recording area. Find a quiet place in your home or apartment where you can consistently record yourself. Even the inside of an open closet can provide the dead recording zone you need for optimal recording. Go to your local electronics store to purchase some foam panels to deaden sound. If you can, set up the recording area nearby to where you work and keep your mike on when you are working at your desk. Have some reading material and scripts ready. Every so often, pop over to the mike and record. Make it a fun part of your work experience—a flight from your daily routine. For more great home studio and location recording information, check out ***The Voice Actor's Guide to Recording at Home and On The Road.by Harlan Hogan and Jeffrey P. Fisher.***

- **Purchase recording equipment.** While you can purchase some of your equipment from local electronics stores such as RadioShack, Guitar Center and in Chicago, Sweetwater, however your best bet is *VoiceOverEssentials.com-the only on-line store specializing in equipment & resources (and a lot of free advice) solely for the voice-over worker.*

    - **Purchase a microphone and cord.** A good studio mike should be at least three hundred dollars or more. Buy two microphone cords. This way you will have a spare if something goes wrong or if you need a second mike for dialogue work with other voice actors.

- **Purchase a microphone stand.** Go for professional quality. There is not that much difference in price, and doing so will mean your setup will approximate the ones in downtown studios. The microphone stand should be for reading standing up. Get used to reading up on your feet. That is how you will record most of the time.

- **Purchase a copy stand.** Again, professional quality is best. Cover it with a small carpet sample. This will get rid of pinging sounds off of the metal stand. It will cost fifty dollars or more for the stand.

- **Purchase an attachable reading light.** A simple clip-on light will work to light up your copy.

- **Purchase a small table.** Place it nearby to hold your water or apple slices that you'll use to keep your mouth from getting dry and making unneeded noises when recording. I will discuss this in further detail later in the book.

Step Six: Practice! But Practice Correctly!

There is no shortcut to being a good voiceover reader. The greats that I knew in this business practiced every day, refining their work and discovering new voices and sounds to offer in auditions. You even need to practice your demo to make sure you are on top of the voices you are offering to prospective clients.

You have to put your time in and read a lot of copy. But it is important to practice correctly! In sports they say to practice right and play right. If you're developing a straight golf shot or an accurate first tennis serve, you have to practice correctly to get the result you desire. The same is true of reading voiceover copy. Develop bad habits and you will develop poor technique for reading copy.

- **Transcribe spots from radio and television and form a script file.** With TiVo and DVR at home, transcribing a commercial is easy:

  1. Tape a few hours of radio or TV.
  2. Get a legal pad and transcribe.
  3. Start a folder on your computer called *VO SCRIPTS*.
  4. Transfer the transcriptions to Word documents on your computer and then place them in the VO SCRIPTS folder.
  5. Keep typing up spots and adding them to this folder over time. After a while you will have a full library of scripts to print out and use for practice and demos. I loved doing this because I got to imitate and master current voices and commercials on the air. Fake it till you make it, as they say.
  6. Go online to Edge Studio and sample the extensive script library there.
  7. Check out ISpotTv.com for the latest spots on the air!!

- **Immerse yourself in a variety of voices from radio, television and the Internet.** This is a big one. It is vitally important to immerse your brain in voices to up your repertoire. YouTube is a great source for this, as are old movies, cartoons, and the like. I always tell my story of imitating a conductor barking out stops on the Hudson River Line to New York. A producer on a national Coors Light spot needed a conductor voice to fill out his TV spot. I did the voice and made some great money for my imitation. This is how most of us start anyway: imitating what we hear for fun. Later it can lead to profit.

- **Listen to commercials that jump out at you—ones that you would love to read.** Let voiceover be a form of play and imitation. Just like you imitate your favorite uncle or cartoon character, read the spots that sound like your voice or that are interesting to read. You are the one practicing, so there is no reason to bore yourself with copy you hate to read.

- **Have your scripts ready to record.** Once you have your recording area set up, place a few scripts on your stand to entice you to practice. Get in front of the microphone, set your levels of recording, and start recording.

- **Cut your script down to size and mark it up.** Think of reading the script in pieces instead of the entire text top to bottom. Start by underlining the client's name so you will give it extra emphasis when you get there. Underline key adjectives and phrases, such as the product's slogan. Underline all prices and product names as well as words like *free*. Then practice each separate piece before reading entire script. This helps you get comfortable with the various copy points and elements of the script. At this point, start doing full reads.

  Here's a sample marked-up script:

  Lupo Rent-A-Car – Thirty-second TV

  When it's time for your next trip,

  Get more / from Lupo Rent-A-Car.

  Low rates?

  Our name / guarantees it.

Quality car selection?

Lupo has / the car for you

That will make / every part of your trip

More memorable.

Have fun in the sun. / Ski / till you drop. / Or travel / to wide-open spaces.

When you're ready / we'll be waiting for you at the airport.

Remember, / next time you book / a rental car

It's time for a Lupo Rent-A-Car.

There are many ways to mark up a script. The one I offer uses slashes to bunch up phrases / so you can think / of the phrases / as single thoughts. This helps you talk in a more natural way and get through the script more easily. There will be more information on this in the "The Script" section.

- **Prepare five to ten different scripts to read.** Read the full script twice. Then redo top lines, tags, and any mistakes. Do not memorize. Move the scripts around and read lines out of order.

- **Read fifteen minutes at a time.** That is all it takes. Don't overdo it.

- **Record and listen later.** You will have fresher ears to critique yourself.

- **Time yourself.** Get a stopwatch and make sure reads are a second or two below the time allowed for the spot.

- **Practice anywhere.** Practice in your car, while walking down the street, or in the elevator—it's all good. I get caught all the time talking to myself trying out voices. People may think you're strange, but it just might get you a job one day, and then you will have the last laugh.

- **Be mindful of the following while practicing:**

  - Don't read the script so much you are memorizing it.
  - Don't do rapid reads one after the other. This disconnects you from the script.
  - Don't get mad over mistakes. Mistakes release you to do better reads at times.
  - Don't overwork your voice.
  - Don't read too slowly. You will get comfortable with slow reads.

Step Seven: Make a Demo

To get represented by an agent or audition online, you need to have a recorded sample of your work. This is called your *voiceover demo.*

- **When is it time?** It's time once you've had enough experience in front of a microphone through classes or actual voiceover work. At this point, you should feel comfortable reading whatever script you are given. In addition, you should be able to course correct: slow down if you are going too fast and hit a different note in the script when directed. Overall, you should feel that you are running your own ship here and staying in control during the session and the audition. If all of this is true, you are ready to start your career.

Remember, however, that you are not a doctor until you get a degree, and you are not an official voiceover performer until you have a demo.

- **How do I get started?**

  - Go online and find out who is known to do great work at a good price.
  - Work with a seasoned demo producer and a top-notch engineer.
  - Travel to a bigger city or find a local engineer who knows how to build spots.
  - Get a range of prices. You may find that it can cost anywhere from a few hundred dollars to many thousands of dollars. Something in the range of $1,500 to $2,500 should be sufficient. Remember, you want a demo that is high quality and will last a few years.
  - Think of what type of work you would like to do: audiobooks, narration, strictly commercial work, animation, or all of the above?
  - If you are in the Chicago area, my partner David Leffel and I produce high quality work producing demos at a good price. Contact at jefflupetin@gmail.com for an estimate.

ULTIMATE VOICEOVER TIP!

It's not how many voices you do but the range of your own voice.

Many of us got into this business to do funny voices and crazy cartoon sounds we loved as kids. However, the voiceover business requires you to master your own voice and how it goes up and down your register. Top casting agent and writer David Lewis preaches this as the key to hiring good voice talent. He regales my classes with practical advice: improve your voice range and don't just do a lot of trick voices.

Practice reading spots up and down in your vocal range. Focus on breath. Focus on maintaining the note of the spot. Focus on reading in this style for all your takes. Sure, trick voices are fun and can be done, too. But unless you have a career in animation, you will need to master your own sound. This is cool and very rewarding.

These are the types of scripts you should record according to your gender and age:

Men

- **Teens to twenties:** Scripts that show high energy and enthusiasm.
- **Twenties to thirties:** Spots about beer, cars, electronics, and fast food as well as dialogue.
- **Thirties to forties:** Similar to Twenties and Thirties with some attitude and authoritative styles thrown in. Insurance, Health commercial reads.
- **Forties to fifties and older:** Mature, deep, resonant, serious, and sophisticated styles. Narration and promo scripts.

Women

- **Teens to twenties:** Bubbly and enthusiastic scripts. There are young announcers for cereal and teen products.
- **Twenties to thirties:** Personal care, household, and food products.
- **Thirties to forties:** All products. Do moms, wives, and sexy sounds.
- **Forties to fifties and older:** Mature sounds. Do older moms and grandmas and scripts for insurance companies and health products.

- **How much should my voiceover demo cost?** Beware of extremely highly priced demo producers. You want to produce a great demo. With proper coaching, great scripts, great engineering, and your marvelous talents, you can. However, there is no reason to spend more than you need to. A good demo should cost you in the range of $1,500 to $2,300.

Things to avoid when searching for a demo producer:

- Avoid those who are not currently working in the business day-to-day.
  This can cause the demo to have a dated sound.
- Avoid lots of flash and lots of promises that add up to an overpriced demo, $3000 and beyond.
- Avoid people who are jacks-of-all-trades and not masters of the intricate art of the voice demo.
- Avoid super-cheap demos. Even with good studios, these can get poor results and cause you to start over.
- Don't allow quick over flattering responses to suck you in. You need accurate assessment, not pandering.

One of my students went the cheaper route and had to work with me, which resulted in his being $900 poorer. Another student was hit for $5000 for lots of recording sessions and a sub quality product that missed the mark. In both cases, more money had to be spent—not a good thing.

- **Who should record my demo?** Please work with someone who is in the business currently and who has a clear knowledge of the business. Your best bet is to work with a current studio engineer who works cutting spots during the day and does demo work as well. Your buddy who is a musician might agree to record you, but he may not know the timing and style necessary for a good demo. It's good for practice but not for a final product. One of my earliest students, **Sonia Hassan**, called me to ask for quick demo pieces for her demo record. I wrote her about five or six pieces and sent them to her. She did terrific reads that got her some quick voiceover work. From that point on, I was on the road to be a demo producer myself.

- **Do the following:**

    - Listen to top agency VO talent from Chicago, New York, and Los Angeles online. Hear the quality you should expect.
    - Get a sample of work the producer has done and match it up, listening for mix quality, voice clarity, and length.
    - If the demo strays way over one minute or so, it is a sign of inexperience.
    - Do an hour of studio time and see if you like the producer's direction and if you mesh while working together.

Got a minute?

That is all the time you need to get started in the voiceover business. Most agents require a minute or more to be featured on their websites. There, you will be listed with all the other actors at your agency.

You can accomplish a lot in a minute to a minute and fifteen seconds. Your voice selections will vary from eight to nine seconds for signature or money reads (reads that best define or use your voice) to three to four seconds for quick bursts to show range or character. Get to the essence of the voice in as little copy as possible. When you record your demo, you should come away with two cuts: one at one minute and one that is just slightly over.

- **Basic flow of a demo:**

1. Opening: Friendly, conversational, and not too loud or too much of a character. This should be a more natural "you" read.

2. Contrast read: Quieter, quicker, lower, and sexier than the first read.
3. Solid money read: The best of your demo pieces. Different energy from the previous read. Your client might stop listening after this point, so it's important that he hears the money read here.
4. Dialogue piece.
5. Character piece.
6. Retail spot high in energy.
7. Another money read but with a twist. Do a different product.
8. Straight-ahead business style.
9. Conversational to act as a bookend like the beginning. The ending can be funny to some extent.

Step Eight: Get an Agent

This is where it gets tricky. To successfully compete in the voiceover business, you have to have an agent. Yet many voice talent can begin and perhaps stay independent by working the Internet market.

The agent is the conduit for scripts, auditions and sessions. The agent also handles getting you paid and keeping up with clients if they are late as well as pitching them the right amount for your voice work. The voice agent also develops a relationship with you so he or she knows what the best spots are for your voice range. And yet…

If you cannot get an agent at first, you can still work the voiceover business by working online casting sites like Voice123, Voices.com, and others. You will submit your demo and receive scripts via the Internet that you can use to record and submit. If you are chosen, they may use the track you sent in or have you rerecord. You will usually be paid via PayPal. Like other nonunion voice actors, you are more at the whim of the client's integrity when it comes to getting paid on time. However, I know many start-up voiceover talent who have developed good relationships with online clients. Overall, it is a great place to begin if agency representation is not a go right now. You can get savvy at sending in well-recorded auditions and developing a client base on your own. There's nothing wrong with that.

My advice would be to develop your online presence first and then get hooked up with an agent. Typically, the auditions will not in any way conflict. Many traditional walls in place in the process of seeking clients have fallen or been altered immeasurably. When I started in VO, if you had an agent, that meant you would work, not just audition. Now the Internet has splintered so much of the work to nonunion actors that it can be the Wild West out there. Some of the biggest acts in music have taken on the job of promoting their own wares and handling their placement. Most indie bands do the same thing. I firmly believe you work harder when it is you at the helm and you who gets the reward totally.

You need to get comfortable with taking action, motivating yourself, and setting goals that can be achieved. Yes, the agent will be a factor in this, but you are responsible for your audition quality, your session work, and other tasks, such as following up and marketing. To get better at all of this, you should read self-improvement literature or attend seminars that address getting past the hurdles that could slow you down.

I love being in charge of myself, knowing my hard work and talent can move me forward. This is a very powerful thing to know and develop in this business. You don't want to be looking outward for others to create your success. That's a bad idea. You don't have to have a type A personality with an overly aggressive attitude. Just be able relate to people and offer great voice choices. That comes with lots of practice and experience. That will let you run your own ship.

- **So how do you get an agent?** Approaching an agent can be a daunting task. But remember, if you have trained and perfected your craft, you have something to offer; you are not a charity case looking for a handout. You have the ability to make your agent money with your voice, so be selective as to the best fit for you. You want to be represented by someone who gets who you are and sees the potential in applying your abilities.

- **At first, ask for feedback, not representation.** You want to sneak up on your agent. Years ago, I learned a valuable lesson: people love to give you their feedback or opinions. At the time, I was diligently trying to get work as a copywriter. To that end, I had created my ad book and called around to ad agencies to get work. I would pick up the phone, dial, and say, "Hi, my name is Jeff Lupetin, and I'm looking for a job as a copywriter."

  "I'm sorry," they would immediately say. "We have no openings now." Then they would hang up.

  This happened for days until I suddenly changed my tact. I called, they answered, and I said, "Hi, my name is Jeff Lupetin, and I'm looking to get some feedback on my ad book. Is there anyone there who could help me?"

  The receptionist's tone changed completely. No longer just wanting to brush me off right away, she became a helpful assistant. "Hold on a second." She would then connect me to an ad writer who was more than willing to give his opinion of my work. I made many visits to Chicago agencies I discovered there was no shortage of people who would spend multiple visits helping me revise my book. This taught me a valuable lesson. By asking for feedback, I had tapped into the universal good will of people helping people.

  The same is true when approaching an agent. Sure, your goal is to get an agent who will send you out on work. But agents are besieged with people sending in CDs and MP3s of their work. Most hit the garbage can hard. By calling an agent and asking him or her for feedback on your demo, he or she gets to be the expert and carefully listen to your work. The agent will be more open to you because you are humbly only asking for feedback and not representation. If your demo is good, the agent may want to rep you or, at the bare minimum, audition you to see how you do. There's nothing wrong with that, is there? Don't hide that you want representation, but look at this as a powerful initial step to getting connected with an agent.

Step Nine: Collect Your Contacts

If I were to list out the most important things in order, I would easily put "collect your contacts" at the top. We have all heard the saying "It's not what you know but who you know." That has some credence in the voiceover business as well.

Get a sheet of paper and write anyone at all who is involved in the ad business, including audio engineers, public relations connections, and freelance writers. Anyone connected can be a conduit to work. Fellow actors, of course, could put a good word in for you at their agency.

A good contact who is well placed in a top agency could be a funnel for work beyond what any agent can provide. In most cases, your agent merely provides opportunity in the form of the audition, while an ad agency connection can provide actual work. In other words, an agent gets you in line whereas a great connection gets you to the front of the line or, better yet, in the door.

If an advertising producer or writer loves the sound of your voice and, more importantly, working with you, you could get immediate approval for a spot. Just make sure you are ready to perform at the level needed for the work.

As I mentioned before, the Internet can spawn a whole client base that you can develop for big gains in your career. Picture sending your demo out as like spreading seed: the more you spread, the more will grow. It is scientific at some point. The energy put into your career with a quality talent base can produce great results. That will come from your hard work and persistence and the marketing tools you use to keep your clients up-to-date and expanding. Every job I have done in my life, from adolescence through adulthood, has come from a connection I had for that work. That should say it all.

Since you are reading my book, write down my name as well!

You may consider temping or interning at a recording studio or ad agency. You might be surprised by how many careers begin with work as a receptionist or intern. Imagine this scenario: You are working as a temp at an ad agency. It is late, and they need someone to voice a few lines in a radio spot. You just happen to be working on your demo, and they have you give it a shot. Voilà! You do a radio spot, get a new piece for your demo, and make a vital connection for work. It happens all the time. You may not get paid at first in these situations—which occur a bit under the radar for legality's sake—but any chance is good. Next time, however, ask to be paid!

ULTIMATE VOICEOVER TIP!

Get in the circle for the best hiring results.

No matter how talented you may be, if people don't know you, you may have a hard time getting noticed. When you are in a circle—at an internship or job—people know you and are therefore more apt to give you an opportunity. Your personality and track record are trusted, and people know you can be relied upon to deliver what they need. They will be willing to give you a shot. I have had this happen to me over and over again. Recently, I have received some directing projects through Chicago Recording Company. They recommended me for a big video game project out of Canada called Watch Dogs. Since I direct students in my classes there at night, I was a known and trusted commodity. When names of possible candidates were bandied about, mine rose to the top.

So, connect, do favors, get to know the people you work with, and most importantly, do good, reliable work.

ULTIMATE VOICEOVER TIP!

Be nice to everyone. Someone you were nice to might just hire you someday.

When I was in college at Northwestern University, I lived just off Noyes Street near the north campus. I used to go to a pharmacy there to buy assorted things. One day, I started a conversation with a young girl named Lisa. She was in high school at the time. We hit it off and started to talk every time I came in there. In the 1980s—years later—I walked into an agency for a job I was hired for and found none other than Lisa Givot sitting at a desk. She was now working as an advertising producer downtown at a big Chicago agency. She smiled and said, "Remember me?" I laughed, happy to see her and grateful I hadn't been a jerk to her back in my college days.

Any intern or secretary may be in the business one day. My agent at Naked Voices, Laurie Haverkamp, was once an intern. Be nice to everyone. It makes for a better work environment in general, and a person you were nice to might hire you someday.

This is a relationship business no matter how good you are at your craft. It is those wonderful people who remember you high atop the city in their offices who make your career what it is. Never forget that. Be kind to those rising up and those coming down a bit. At the bare minimum, this will make you feel great and love your work, and it will create a great environment to work in. What is so bad about that?

Step Ten: Tell Your Story and Let Them Know You Are Open for Business

"Hey, Jeff. What's up?" Oh, the same old. That's an opportunity missed! Tell friends and associates what you are really up to. If you don't tell your story, even your closest friends might not be able to hook you up with connections they may have.

Not all of us like to toot our own horn or brag about our exploits. However, it is vital to be honest and inform the world of what you are doing voiceover wise so that opportunities can arise for you. You just never know who knows who in this business.

To that end, you should come up with a realistic story of what you are doing that includes details like who you have studied with and who is doing your demo. It will make you feel like a pro even if the work has not come in yet. Remember, you are laying the groundwork for your career. Once you have a voice demo and you hit the phones, this story will keep you from rambling on. If you are in transition from a different profession to this one, just say you are focusing on voiceover work. Many people will give you funny stares if you tell them you are looking to be in the VO profession full-time. This is a part-time profession that requires full-time attention. To succeed it has to be a consistent part of your life, but at the same time it can't supply all your income and act as your only daily source of work.

Years ago I started doing spoken-word stories and comedy. I wanted others to know this. I went to an industry party and decided to focus on discussing this new passion. I spoke with a woman named Marssie Mencotti. Marssie teaches voiceover for the radio department at Columbia College in addition to being a very funny actress.

She asked me if I would like to be part of an evening of radio drama at the school. As I am prone to do, I said yes immediately. I did the evening and played Sherlock Holmes. It was a success, and I got to meet others in the department like Mary Martucci and Barbara Calabrese, the head of the department. Long story short, I was asked to develop a class called Voice for Animation for the school. I am teaching there now all because I made the initial effort to tell my story. The dividends keep coming in.

Before that, I was hired as an actor by the Falcon Picture Group head, Carl Amari, to be on *The Twilight Zone* radio show. This is a national show that recreates the original scripts for radio. Once I had established a relationship with Carl, I always wanted to work for him on a bigger project. As we got to know each other, I kept asking to be a part of a project he was doing. Finally, in 2009, I got the chance.

Carl had produced a series called *The Word of Promise New Testament* starring many big Hollywood actors and local folk like me. Now he wanted to do a teenage version called *The Next Generation* and asked if I wanted to direct. I said yes despite knowing very little about the Bible. But I dove in, and later in the year, I received an Audie Award for direction. The engineer on that project was a talented musician/engineer named Sean McKie..years later he called me from the coast to see if I wanted to work at a new newsmovie company called TouchVision. I was soon hired. If not for my time at TouchVision, I never would have completed this book. How about that!!

This proves that planting the seed works but also that what is most important is being in the circle and being trusted to do good work. This method works over and over. You can't beat it!

The other must for aspiring voice talent is having a website. A website shows that you are here to stay and that you are open for business. It proves your legitimacy. To me it says that you investing your time, energy, and money into a new venture. You are not fly-by-night but the real deal.

Your website should have the following:

1. Your Commercial VO demo
2. Other demos, including characters, narrations, promos and trailers, and audiobooks.
3. Full commercials if you want.

4. A graphic that sells your image or at least boldly states your name.
5. Contact information so that a client can reach you (agent's phone number, your phone number, etc.).

Your website can be made immediately. There are various ways to approach this process. I would recommend hiring someone who is in this business and can get your material hosted via GoDaddy or another service. My demo was done by Dan Manas of Best Light Productions. I get the greatest compliments for it. It is money well spent!

ULTIMATE VOICEOVER TIP!

A head shot is not needed for a VO website.

No, you are not hideously ugly, and no, you are not so beautiful that the sight of you will blind clients to your voiceover talents. The reality is simply that you don't want a client to typecast you. If you are young, old, or in between, your image might place a thought in the client's mind about you when you should be keeping them guessing.

I call it the "picture in the pizza parlor" theory. In my local pizza parlor, there are autographed pictures of the DJs and other celebrities on the local radio. When I see their headshots, I think about how I never would have imagined that that was the person I was listening to everyday. It is weird. You might seem too young, too big, or too small—who the heck knows? So while you can include an image of yourself (a caricature perhaps), you should not include a headshot. If you are using the website to host your on-camera portfolio as well, then have them click on the "Acting" section before they see any head shots. Let a voiceover client hear your wonderful voice first so that he or she doesn't eliminate you because you look like a cousin who pushed him or her off a cliff as a youngster.

Certain keywords will make your website come up when it's being searched for online. For instance, if you search for "voiceover teaching," my site will come up. It is a global market now. My friend and editor Joe Wallace had someone reach out to him from Japan for a job that he was right for. You never know. Once you have an agent, he or she can link your website to the agency website so you can get double the exposure. The website is good to create before you have representation to create a link to potential clients. You can simply direct connections to your site, and they can listen in the comfort of their home or office.

This material will be reiterated in the next section, "Start-Up Costs," with some other more detailed information.

Step Eleven: Show Some Gratitude

So much of being successful in this business has to do with your mind-set. An attitude of gratitude really helps in this regard. You need a lot of help to get going in this business. It is a process. So each recommendation, each person listening to your demo, and each person you audition for and work for later plays a part. If you can develop an attitude where you feel each tiny contribution means something, you will be awash in good feelings about all the factors working in your favor. Conversely, if you always feel it is about how you either get the job or don't, you will be disappointed most of the time. That is a fact because you will get a very small percentage of what you audition for no matter how talented you are in this business. No matter how good your voice, it just may not be the sound they want.

As I mentioned before, I had such a competitive attitude when I began in the voiceover business. It did not serve me well. When I learned to be grateful for even auditions, I started to relax more and became more upbeat about the ups and downs of the work I was doing. Realizing how great it was to have an agent and to be able to work in this business, I became more at ease and willing to take what came day-by-day.

After a while, when the work started flowing in, it seemed like I was receiving an embarrassment of riches. My feeling of gratitude for even the smallest part of the business put me in an open place, which drew work to me in abundance.

This switch of mind-set from “kill or be killed” competition to one of gratitude and service took a lot of work to establish and maintain, of course. I read books on positive thinking that really changed my life. I had to keep cleaning out the disgruntled feelings, which are easier to have, and replacing them with lighter, grateful ones. It’s not easy—it’s like cleaning off your kitchen table in a windstorm. It takes work, but what doesn’t if it is an important part of your life? The voiceover business changed my life, but I had to start thinking about gratitude and abundance instead of lack. It definitely worked, but I still have to keep replacing negative thoughts with positive ones to keep going. This is a great place to start when approaching the voiceover business. Work to keep a positive attitude and be grateful for all that takes place. It really can be a miracle at times. Enjoy!

PART I: Getting Started

SUMMARY

I just shared *a lot* of information with you. I don't expect you to remember it all. Most of what you just read might even be flying out of your head right now. This book won't disintegrate. Keep referring back to this information over time to review what I shared with you. But just in case it is needed, here is a quick review of the vital needs for getting started:

- ✓ Read out loud a lot.
- ✓ Get taught by a quality VO pro
- ✓ Take a class in improvisation.
- ✓ Make a demo with an experienced pro
- ✓ Buy recording equipment for practice and for sending in auditions.
- ✓ Work your business contacts for potential work.
- ✓ Stay humble and be grateful for it all.

PART II

Upfront Needs and Costs

Before we get started, let's do an inventory of what you should already have regarding equipment. Here are some basic needs:

- Computer, laptop, or desktop.
- Dedicated work area.
- Microphone.
- Headphones.
- Recording software.

That is a good place to start. You can start small and inexpensive but should always work to get the best. As you start making some good money, upgrade your computer and microphone. The better you sound, the better the chance of higher-paying voiceover work.

As I mentioned earlier, this is the voiceover business, not the voiceover charity. There is an up-front and continual cost to competing at a high level in the voiceover business. What I will do in this section is give you some parameters and plans to work with so you can handle the financial costs of getting started.

First let's talk about the practice/recording area.

Practice/Recording Area

You need a place to practice honing the techniques I am offering in this book. Just like you would have a work desk for a hobby or any other avocation you may have, setting aside a dedicated spot for your voiceover work is key. The area will be where you practice and record as well as where you store your scripts. It should not be used for other activities like paying bills. You want it to be a voiceover haven that is away from the other parts of your life—a new special place that is fun to visit again and again. What does that look like?

- **Simple: Table in closet.**

  Get a small table, push your clothes to the side, and create a good soundproof place to practice and record. Make sure there are no moth balls in there…Ha-ha. For younger students living in an apartment setup, this will do. Just make sure the table can handle a microphone and your laptop or desktop and you have somewhere to hold your scripts. Recording in the middle of the room is going to attract ambient noise (heat vents, dogs barking, people walking around, etc.). You might consider using an old moving blanket to further muffle the sounds. This is an easy way to begin.

  - **Use:** For practice and sending in voiceover auditions. It's not the best for producing final work for the air.

- **Better: Desk in sun porch or extra bedroom.**

  Many old apartments have sun porches that function as places for guests to crash or to keep bikes out of the snow. The city of

Chicago and other cities are full of them. Drape some moving blankets or regular blankets to muffle sound and set up your desk there. You will have a little more room than if you just stuck your desk in a closet. If you have the luxury of having a spare guest room, think of setting up your equipment there for an isolated recording space It doesn't need to take up the entire room, unless that room already serves as a business office for you. But in this scenario, remember to keep your recording space separate, not mixed with personal or financial matters. In my basement office, my mike and equipment are at the opposite end of the room from my laptop.

- **Use:** Practice and sending in auditions. With proper sound baffling, it can work for final production for the air.

Best: Home recording studio.

Check out ***The Voice Actor's Guide to Recording at Home and On The Road.*** **by Harlan Hogan and Jeffrey P. Fisher.** Renowned voiceover artist Harlan Hogan has captured the market of the dos and don'ts of setting up a home studio. A home studio can be a source of pride for a voiceover professional and a place where they can record copy that is good enough for the air or final production use. In this scenario, you will be able to practice, record, and produce voiceover copy that can be used by your client. For the beginner and those on a limited budget, this may be shooting a bit high, but Harlan offers ideas to make even this highest-end option more affordable ***Harlan Hogan's VoiceOver Essentials.com sells acoustic foam lined Porta-Booths®. These lightweight devices fold for storage and travel and when you put mic inside it "hears" and acoustically reinforced space.*** **This is a great go-to site to establish a great recording environment at a good price.** ***VoiceOverEssentials.com - is the only on-line store specializing in equipment & resources (and a lot of free advice) solely for the voice-over worker.***

Use: For practice, sending in auditions, and producing quality voiceover work.

Be diligent about the sound quality of your area. If you live in the city, beware of public transportation noise or horns and sirens. You may be used to the sounds and not notice them, but they will be recorded and become unnecessary background noise. In the suburbs, bird sounds could creep in if you are near a window. Send out some samples to an experienced VO person (even me) to judge the quality.

Privacy

No matter where you practice and record, you need to develop a comfortable environment. You don't want to be self-conscious about how you might be disturbing anyone in your living space or the neighbor on the other side of the wall. This is something new for you, and you have to get comfortable with sending in auditions. You want your reads to be relaxed and fun. If my wife or kids walk in, I might get distracted or pull back. It might even seem odd to be doing weird new voices in the basement office by yourself.

Establish a routine where family members and friends are not hovering around making you self-conscious. Comfort level at home and in the studio is key for success.

Equipment

Next I will cover the cost of equipment necessary to practice and record.

- **Computer.** As I mentioned before, you may or should already have some equipment necessary to get started in your life. A good, fast computer is one of those necessities. Be it a laptop or a desktop, a MacBook or a PC, this is where you will be doing your recording.

As of this writing, a new MacBook can cost around $1,500 for a 13.3-inch screen and $2,500 for a 17-inch screen. That is what I am using, and I love it! A PC can range from under $1,000 to $1,500 or so. There is a little more flexibility in price with a PC. I would recommend having a laptop because it is portable and you can take it with you and send in auditions no matter where you roam. Audio files don't eat up as much hard drive space as video files, so you don't have to have a super-high capacity, but if your laptop is over five years old, you may want to upgrade your memory.

- **File Protection.** Make sure you have quality backup for your files. With PCs, viruses can wreak havoc on your material. You do not want to be sending infected files out to clients. Make sure you are diligent about virus protection and keep updating as you go along. Also, back up your files with external hard drives or inexpensive services like Carbonite. Computers can be lost, stolen, and ruined in many ways. Don't go through the heartbreak and inconvenience of lost files and materials. I had my iMac stolen out of my house and lost a lot of shots I will never see again. I now have Carbonite, which automatically backs up all my files offline. It can cost as little as fifty-nine dollars a year. If the worst were to happen, I will get all my materials right back. Phew.

- **Software.** Your computer will need some recording software to record your fine voiceover tracks. There are a variety of software programs out there. Let's start with the ones that are free.

  Audacity. Audacity is free, open-source software for recording and editing sounds. It is available for Mac OS X, Microsoft Windows and others.
  Audacity is free software and a good place to start. Just download it to your computer and off you go. It is easy to use and can be learned in a short period of time.

Lots of my students start here and gravitate toward other costlier options. But in the beginning, let there be Audacity.

GarageBand. Garage Band is a free software application that comes with Mac OS X and can also be used on IOS. It allows users to create music and podcasts. It is developed by Apple as a part of the iLife software package.

Sound Forge. This costs $300 or more. Sony Sound Forge (formerly known as *Sonic Foundry Sound Forge*) is a digital audio-editing suite by Sony Creative Software that is aimed at the professional and semiprofessional markets.

A limited version sold as *Sound Forge Audio Studio* provides an inexpensive entry-level digital audio editor; it was formerly known as *Sonic Foundry's Sound Forge LE.*

The software initially had Windows 3.x support, but after version 3.0, all sixteen-bit support was dropped. Additionally, Windows 95 support was dropped after Sound Forge 5.0.

- **Pro Tools.** At this writing, Pro Tools costs $300 to $400 and can be downloaded. It is a digital audio workstation for Mac OS X and Microsoft Windows operating systems developed and manufactured by Avid Technology. It is widely used by professionals throughout the audio industries for recording and editing in music production, film, and television post-production. Pro Tools can run as stand-alone software or operate using a range of external A/D converters and internal PCI or PCIe audio cards with onboard DSP.

  Pro-Tools may be bundled with a mixer called an Mbox or an Mbox Mini (the latter has less inputs). I purchased an Mbox for around $1,000, and the software Pro Tools came with it.. They also often throw in a free DVD tutorial on how to use the system. *At this writing, you may have the ability to use Pro-Tools without an M-box. Technology keeps changing at a rapid pace.*

So you can see there are a variety of prices and options when it comes to software packages. To keep costs low at the start, you might want to start with Audacity and Garage Band if you have a Mac. Otherwise, move up to the industry standards and use Sound Forge or Pro Tools.

- **Recording setup.** Your basic necessities to get started recording at home are as follows:

    - Microphone.
    - Microphone stand.
    - Copy stand.
    - Light.
    - Pop shield.
    - Headsets.
    - Audio monitor speakers.

You want to have a setup that is similar to those in recording studios. It may not be as expensive, but it will get you comfortable so that when you go to a studio, it is not such a different setup for you to record copy.

I will describe some basic choices and name their prices to give you a sense of the upfront cost for getting set up to record.

ULTIMATE VOICEOVER TIP!
Spend the most money on a good microphone and then invest in a good demo.

This is a no-brainer move here. First, having a high-quality microphone will help ensure your auditions and home productions have a top-end sound. You don't have to spend downtown studio money, but securing a great mike will reap dividends in the long run. Secondly, spending extra to be with an accomplished demo producer is always worth it. He or she will typically be mixing spots during the day and know exactly what the current hot sound is. He or she will not use old, worn background music or sound effects. The producer will create a modern soundscape in which your voice will shine. I have done this all along in my career. What it does is it gives you a demo that sounds like it was taken right off the air. The appearance that you are national quality talent goes a long way to get you work. Just make sure you keep practicing so you are ready when your moment arrives.

- **Microphones.** There are a wide variety of microphones to choose from when setting up your recording area. I will present a few popular ones that have been used extensively by voice talent. By all means, consult with experienced voice talent and see what they like. You can make it very easy on yourself by just piggybacking on a savvy voice talent's research about microphones. If you are more of a tech geek and like to talk and try out all kinds of microphones, then let that be your path. All roads lead to you being an informed and well-set-up voiceover talent.

- **Simple: USB microphone.** A USB microphone has a cord that connects right into a USB port on your computer.

The Blue Yeti by Blue Microphones, available at Amazon, many times for $100 or less. This is a versatile USB mike with three condenser capsules and four polar pattern settings. It is really easy to work with, basically plug it in to our USB port and off you go! Its features are as follows:

- Master volume.
- Mute button.
- Proprietary tri capsule array.
- Mike gain control.
- Zero-latency headphone output with amplifier and volume control.
- USB mini jack.
- Standard threaded mike stand mount.
- Custom base with cable management.

You Tube features links that show the mike in use. I find it to be a terrific low cost option at the start of your career or use as a second microphone for the road. I recommend it to all my students and their feedback has been very positive.

- **Better: Dynamic microphone.** Dynamic microphones work via electromagnetic induction, using the same dynamic principle as in a loudspeaker except reversed. A small movable induction coil, positioned in the magnetic field of a permanent magnet, is attached to the diaphragm. When sound enters through the windscreen of the microphone, the sound wave moves the diaphragm. When the diaphragm vibrates, the coil moves in the magnetic field, producing a varying current in the coil through electromagnetic induction. They are sturdy, full-sound mikes that are relatively inexpensive and hold up well over time. Their ability to handle high-gain situations before encountering feedback makes them the perfect choice for basic home recording and onstage use.

  A common type is the Shure SM58, which costs ninety-nine dollars and up. The Shure SM58 might be your choice if you are doing recordings of different types. For instance, you might be in a band and use the microphone for singing in addition to using it for voiceover script recording.

The AKG D 112, which costs $199 and up, is also good for multiple usages but especially good for deeper bass response. Low-frequency voice and instruments will pop through stronger and not require their gain to be raised as high in a mix situation. It's a better mike with a deeper sound, and that is reflected in the higher cost.

Unlike with condenser microphones, no battery or phantom power source is needed for the operation of dynamic microphones.

- **Best: Condenser microphone.** Condenser microphones span from telephone transmitters to inexpensive karaoke microphones to high-fidelity recording microphones in the finest recording studios. They produce a high-quality audio signal and are now the popular choice for voice recording and recording studio applications.

  Their high-end usage is due to their inherent sensitivity requiring very small mass to be moved by the incoming sound wave, unlike other microphone types that require the sound wave to do more work. Unlike dynamic or USB microphones, condenser mikes require a power source, which is provided via microphone inputs on equipment as phantom power or from a small battery. Power is necessary for establishing the capacitor plate voltage and is also needed to power the microphone's electronics.

  The price of condenser microphones vary greatly, but here are a few choices to consider:

  - Good: RØDE NT1-A. This costs around $250. Many come with a pop shield and shock mount.
  - Better: Neumann TLM 102. This costs around $700.
  - Best: Miktek CV4. This costs around $1,300.

> If money is not an issue and you want the very best, a large-diaphragm tube mike is your answer. Miktek CV4 gives you amazing warmth of voice and extreme versatility. Voice or music, this one is a winner. Others in its class include se Electronics Gemini II, MXL Revelation, and Neumann U 47. Check out the website Recording Hacks for live demonstrations of each one of these three.

If you are looking for supreme portability and the lowest cost and highest quality way to practice and send in scripts for auditions, I would recommend a digital recorder. About the size of a pack of cards and very easy to transport, a digital recorder gives you a recording option when you need to send auditions in from home or on the road.

Sony, Tascam, and others make the recorders. The one I have been using and have been recommending is the Zoom H2. This costs around $150 online and is a stereo recorder. It has been used for interviews for years and has recently found its way into the hands of voiceover artists. It's a fun way to get started, especially for new students on a limited budget. I purchased mine off the Sam Ash website.

The H2 and the higher-model H4 can take your original larger WAVE file and convert it to a useable MP3 to send out to your agent or voiceover client. It does it all internally, and then you merely have to connect to your USB port and send the file to your desktop and out to the world. Pretty slick, as my dad would say.

For additional noise protection, you could use the mike stand and pop filter cover. These keep you from getting motion sound when the recorder is handheld. It has a stereo component, so if you are interviewing someone, it handles input on both sides of the microphone. Using the pop filter does just that: eliminates pop or other annoying mouth sounds.

You might also consider the following ideas:

- **Smartphone voice memos.** There it is, right on your smartphone: the voice memo utility. Man, is this easy or what? Simply hit record, speak, and then hit stop. You can instantly send the file via e-mail to your agent. Just know where your mike is on the phone (at the bottom left usually) and don't move it around or talk right into it. Talk across to prevent popping issues.

  I like to read scripts at my desk and save my recordings as voice memos. It gives me a quick sense of what I sound like before going over to my normal RØDE mike. In a jiffy, this kicks butt.

- **PCM recorder app by Tascam.** This is also as easy as the proverbial apple pie. After downloading the PCM recorder app, simply hit record and then send in your file. This differs in that you have volume control so you can bootleg music and not be over modulated. (Did I just tell you to bootleg music? Nah.) Just use it to practice and send in quick voice samples. It's cool stuff. My buddy and demo partner David Leffel turned me on to this...Way to go, David.

- **I-Audition app.** It's a good thing it took me so long to write this book because I would not have otherwise listed this great app. For $4.99, iAudition lets you edit on-screen, which is not the case with the other choices I have listed above. This will come in handy for longer reads. Go through the simple tutorial, and you'll be all set.

If using a voice memo utility, talk a little across or below your phone's microphone and hold the phone steady in your hand to reduce excess sound. Otherwise you will get annoying bursts of breath and mike noise. These voice memo functions work well as a quick way to send in an audition or voice sample when you are out of town or at work.

- **Other recording equipment.** To fill out your recording setup, here are some prices for auxiliary equipment needed to set up your recording space.

    - **Microphone stand boom.** Onstage stands cost approximately eighty-five dollars online at Sweetwater. One of these will suspend your microphone in front of your copy stand. Suspending your mike prevents motion noise from a handheld. You should never record handheld if you can avoid it. Work to have a stationary microphone for best quality.

    - **Copy stand.** A standard Manhasset music stand will cost approximately seventy dollars online at Sweetwater. This stand will hold your copy as you read. It looks like the common music stand found in orchestras and at concerts.

ULTIMATE VOICEOVER TIP!

Get a carpet piece for your copy stand to muffle sound when reading.

Go to a carpet store and find a carpet sample sized for your copy stand. Many carpet stores have these in a stack somewhere. If you went with a wood copy stand, never mind.

One of the fun things about setting up your space is figuring out how to make it safe from other sounds. Ideas come from near and far. This from my editor and voiceover talent Joe Wallace: "You might need to invest in an inexpensive Japanese-type screen from a local store, (the fabric ones are cheaper and more durable than paper) and cover it with a blanket to get a more neutral acoustic quality. I did that, and it worked great for me!"

Good idea, Joe! A simple moving blanket draped over a screen or mounted from the wall can do the trick. The solutions range from simple to complex. You can put a towel or light blanket over yourself like when you inhale Vicks vaporub when you have a cold. Harlan Hogan also has foam box covers for your microphone that should do the trick. Try these out.

Remember, you don't have to spend thousands of dollars or even hundreds. Simple solutions do the trick.

- **Copy stand light.** A Manhasset M57 model costs twenty dollars on Sweetwater. It is a A quality light that attaches to the top of a copy stand to make scripts easier to read.

- **Pop filter with gooseneck.** An onstage pop filter costs approximately forty-five dollars on Sweetwater. The circular pop filter sits in front of your microphone to lessen breath noise and popping sounds when you speak. The gooseneck allows you to adjust to the proper alignment.

- **Headphones.** Sony closed studio headphones cost approximately one hundred dollars on Sweetwater. Good headphones are a must for accurately assessing your vocal quality during recording. There are a variety of styles and quality products here. This is one in the medium range that will get the job done.

ULTIMATE VOICEOVER TIP!

At first, don't use headphones during recording.

Back in the old days of voiceover, headphones were not used. Announcers doing live radio shows did not have earphones, and this practice later carried into the recording studios. You get a less self-conscious or more "on" sound this way. This works especially well when you are just a regular character, as in a "person on the street" scenario. When you want to texture your voice—to make it deeper or quieter perhaps—plop those babies on and hear the magnificence of your voice.

For newbies, headphones create distractions like breath and mouth noise. In the beginning, you can get bothered by this and wonder if you are doing something wrong. You are not. You just need to get used to the sound of your own voice. I still hear my voice on a voice message and wonder how in the heck I ever got into this business. Any breathing noise will be edited out during recording, so it's not an issue.

- **Audio monitor speakers.** M-Audio five-inch active monitors cost approximately three hundred dollars on Sweetwater. After you record your auditions or practice sessions, it is a good idea to hear your voice magnified in this way. You get to hear richness you would not otherwise. It is worth the expense if you have the cash.

ULTIMATE VOICEOVER TIP!

On the other hand, you can use old computer speakers to save a few dollars on monitor speakers.

Why the heck not? When I set up my recording area, I realized that the only thing missing was a good set of speakers for playback. So I went up to my daughter's room and unplugged her Dell computer's desktop speakers and plugged them into my M-box. I was amazed at how good the sound was and never bought the more expensive monitor speakers. This is just a thought among many I offer in this book. If you want the better speakers and money is no object, fire away. The sound I have is perfect for my teaching and audition playback needs.

The fact that my daughter wouldn't be able to hear out of her computer did not deter me in any way. Actually, she has a MacBook now and does not need the speakers. I just wanted to clear that up.

In-studio monitors are things of beauty. The quality and shading of your voice will make you want to run out and buy the best. However, this is the least important of your purchases. I have a set of Bose computer speakers. They rock for voice and music once I convert my AIFF or WAVE files to MP3s and transfer them to my computer. But for simple playback, the speakers purloined from my daughter remain my choice.

Other Start-Up Costs

Training

- Classes and coaching.
- Individual coaching.
- Demo production.
- Website design and hosting.
- Joining the unions AFTRA and SAG.

Classes and Coaching

Beginner and intermediate voiceover classes will cost $350 to $400. As mentioned earlier in this chapter, it is important to get proper training by qualified professionals who can take you through the step-by-step learning process of this profession.

If you come to Chicago, work with me, my partner in demo production, Dave Leffel, or both of us through the demo production stage.

One of the main reasons I started teaching, besides the obvious one that I love to do it, is that I wanted my students to study with teachers who have done a lot of VO work. Many times that is not the case and you just get general comments and sometimes even discouragement that can sink your ship before it takes off from the dock.

If you want to learn this trade, I will teach you. It is worthwhile on many fronts. Just learning how to express yourself by reading aloud is very valuable by itself—a great byproduct of speaking in front of a microphone.

A good class with a great instructor will establish and sharpen your skill set so you can run your own ship when you step before a mike. That is my ultimate goal for you: to train you to handle the process of auditioning and recording and to make changes and adjustments with ease, often before you are directed to do so. It is well worth the money.

Individual Coaching

Three to five lessons of individual coaching will cost approximately four hundred dollars. Individual coaching zones you in on your reads. With a good instructor, you can get through more scripts, learning the different styles one by one. This also fast-forwards you to being ready to do your demo reel. I can tell after a session or two when you will be ready to go. It is usually indicated by your ability to quickly jump into or be directed to the right tone of the spot. If it takes a while, you need further coaching and follow-up practice.

Coaching will help you do the following:

1. Focus in your reading style.
2. Create different reading styles.

3. Transition from louder stage reading to quieter microphone reading.
4. Handle your attitude in front of a microphone.
5. Develop voices for different platforms: commercials, narration, promos, and animation.
6. Become a better, more confident speaker in general.

I am teaching people to handle their thoughts. I am teaching to serve each copy piece like an hors d'oeuvre at a party. You should see the line, let us taste it, and then move on to the next. I recently worked with two on-air news people. They mentioned to me how they read their copy quicker and easier now and with more meaning. This is a surprising byproduct of our time together.

There is no secret to reading well. You just need to know what to do and do it a lot. Practice, practice, practice!

Voiceover Pro Formula for Success:
Great coaching + great demo + great equipment = great professional

This is what you should spend your money on: getting with a great coach, buying quality equipment—particularly your microphone—and then making a killer demo to show you off.

Demo Production

This is your voiceover diploma. It tells prospective agents you are for real, a talent investing in his or her abilities.

Getting your demo produced can be a joyous event, the coming-out party after all the classes and the work you have done on your own to learn this craft. Remember, the voiceover business is harder than it looks but easier than you make it. You need to learn that along the way.

When you are ready to record your demo, it is important to be with a reputable producer.

Prices vary widely from bargain-basement to overpriced, but a good-quality demo, as of this writing, should be around $2500.00. That price accounts for a good coach, an engineer, a studio to record in, appropriate scripts to show off your voice, and hard copies of your final product. If you pay a lot more, it will be overkill for this process. If you pay a lot less, you will get something done, but most likely, as you improve, you will have to invest further money in an upgraded demo.

Here are some reasons why you should get a top-quality demo producer:

1. You will sound exactly like talent that is currently on the air.
2. Your demo will have a longer shelf life, cutting costs over the years.
3. Your material and music will be current to today's market.
4. You may obtain access to auditions coming through the producer's studio.
5. You will have your voice cleaned up and polished by the pro.
6. You will be viewed as a professional even if you're early in your career.

This really is a no-brainer. The extra money I spent going with Jeff Van Steen, my first demo producer, in 1983 really paid off. Jeff's professionalism moved my demo among the big people of the business. While I had some experience with voiceover at that point, I was still new to the business and needed a top demo to propel me. My concept was "Gang of Voices" with my voices auditioning for me at a studio. This comedic concept presented me in a different way than most beginner demos. It was very well received at the agency level and among my peers. It made an instant impact and help jump-start my voiceover career.

I have some good horror stories. One of my students worked with some East Coast producer on a demo that cost in excess of $5000. It was too long and too unfocused and did not show her off in any way. She had not been coached enough to do quality reads, and it showed. The reads were similar in sound and speed and just not that interesting to hear. This was money down the drain. Remember the formula given above:

Another student went the cheap route and got what she paid for: a low-cost demo with boring music and a boring mix: a bad picture frame around an untrained student. She was out $900 and came to us to get coached and produce a high-octane demo. A voiceover demo done too early captures you in an untrained way, like a model without makeup. You need to be ready to do a demo, and you can know you are after you have done all of the following:

1. Taken at least two classes with quality VO professionals.
2. Been coached for your demo, finding and honing your own voice style.
3. Established a practice routine of your own.
4. Learned what types of voices sell (by watching TV and listening to the radio).
5. Learned how to follow directions to shift reads in speed and tone.
6. Learned how to feel confident in front of a microphone doing ad copy.
7. Learned how to elevate a read once in front of a mike.

I won't record you for a demo if I feel you are not ready. You are like a kid on a bicycle: if I am still holding you up, I am doing you no favors. I need to know you can use my coaching to elevate your read to greater creative heights. When you are doing this, you are ready.

As the old commercial used to say, "get the job done right...the first time!"

ULTIMATE VOICEOVER TIP!

Get a commercial demo and a mini narration demo done at the same time.

A commercial demo contains announce styles and character reads found on current radio and television spots. The next area for you will be narration styles. These could range from website pieces for a new company to corporate image videos, to narration for TV shows. It runs the gamut. If you can swing it for a bit more, record your commercial demo and then record three pieces or so for your narration demo. It should not cost double, and it will get you more auditions for work you will have an easier time scoring.

The commercial demo should run just over one minute with the mini narration demo going about the same with less pieces and longer copy. It should show a long form of your reading style found in the commercial reel. This will get two distinct types of work in front of an agent and, hopefully, get you auditions in both areas. The more circles you can handle, the better.

If you have a child or teen who would like to enter the voiceover business then get a demo cut that has less pieces and is way less expensive. The simple reason is that his or her voice will be niched into certain reads:

- The son or daughter.
- The boyfriend or girlfriend.
- Simple announce reads.

This is because your son or daughter's voice will change. There is no need to invest heavily in an eight-year-old's sound that will change soon.

It's like buying expensive baby clothes: they'll soon be outgrown. As you get into your twenties or so, the voice will anchor for a while. That will be the time to expand outward to different reading styles and thus pay more.

There is not as much work for younger children and teens as adults, but a great kid or teen can really come in and clean up if he or she takes direction well and has a fun sound. I teach children's seminars with my fellow VO actor-coach, Deb Doetzer. There are lots of great kids out there!

Remember: get the greatest quality at the lowest possible price.

ULTIMATE VOICEOVER TIP!

Rent an hour of studio time to get better on the microphone while recording.

Before your demo, you might consider getting some quality voiceover scripts and finding a quality recording studio in which to record a few things. The more practice you get in studio, the better you will be as talent. I had the blessing of learning my craft in the studios while working, but if that is not your story, rent an hour and read and record some pieces. You will get a better idea of what you sound like and what you can and cannot handle at this time interpretation wise. Eventually, do some dialogue with a fellow voice actor. Perhaps you can even split the time.

If you are in college, get a shift at the local radio station. This is where I began at Northwestern. I couldn't deal with cotton-mouth when I began but got used to it over time. There may also be indie radio sites you can look into like the Chirp Project here in Chicago. In addition, a personal podcast might be fun to do to get your chops up.

While this differs in focus from actual VO work due to the lack of time restraint and a product to sell, it can help you discover and anchor your basic reading style. It gets you in front of a microphone and comfortable talking to it. Give it a shot.

Website Production and Hosting

This is not something you need right away, but it will be valuable for hosting your demo and related material. Like with a good microphone, the prices here can fluctuate wildly. I would recommend just starting with a simple page design with your name spelled out in an attractive font or a fun graphic that expresses who you are as a person and voiceover talent. Once you are represented by an agent, you will post your commercial and other demos on his or her site. However, a personal site will allow you to post other material not found on your agent reel, such as:

- Shorter or longer versions of your commercial demo.
- Full script reads of commercials.
- Original material of your own, like spoken-word recordings or anything else.

This allows you to not be confined by your agency's website. You can post whatever you like, but keep it clean, OK?

Build Your Own Website

If you have a knack for composition and graphics or would like to learn, you can find templates online for sites, such as at Websites.com. It doesn't hurt to try. My son has put together sites on his own for his music, and it seems to work out fine. Here are some basic dos and don'ts:

1. Create a simple graphic that says who you are. It could be just your name in an interesting font, or it could be a person doing a somersault on the beach. Just make it something easy to look at, fun, and to the point.

2. Avoid noisy or distracting background graphics.
3. Keep your contact info easy to see and use clean, clear type.
4. Don't used hackneyed images like 1940s-style PA mikes.
5. Make buttons that bring visitors to your demos easy to find.
6. Create a graphic or type that is transferable to other platforms like business cards, coffee cups, and anything else you can think of.

Think Steve Jobs and his streamlined, crisp designs for the Mac and the iPhone. There is no better person to copy than the master of modern technology design. Emphasize easy access and colorful, fun graphics.

ULTIMATE VOICEOVER TIP!

Work with and hire experienced professionals versed in the voiceover business to further your success.

I have never been a big fan of being a jack-of-all-trades and a master of none. Those whom I have seen try to handle all aspects of talent, engineering, and graphics usually have strengths in only maybe one of the areas. That goes for the business side of voiceover as well. People who are really creative are seldom the best business people. That is why it is important to have an agent who can handle getting you paid and at the right price.

I have benefited greatly by hiring professionals in all of the above areas. Yes, it costs more, but how much do I lose when my graphics are amateurish and the sound of my demo is average at best? It says a lot. You also have the benefit of employing quality professionals and helping them make a living doing what they do best. This is not a do-or-die choice—just my experience and what I feel strongly about when it comes to setting up your voiceover business. I believe in practice right, play right. You need to be zoned in on all levels to be at a professional grade. This is my goal for you, to compete as a professional. If you don't have a lot of funds to begin, get good coaching to help you learn how to refine your reads. Then move on to a quality mike and eventually a great demo to place you in the voice market. Just build it right each step along the way!

You can find aspiring talent in all areas coming out of the local universities and colleges nearby. An up-and-coming graphic designer, web designer, or engineer may be willing to work at a reduced cost to get experience. That's not a bad way to go.

Hiring a Professional

My websites cost about $2,000 each. If you check out loopytalk.com and ultimatevoiceover.com, you will find quality graphics and design housing my range of voices and teaching techniques.

I continue to get great traffic, especially to my teaching site, and great comments for both. That means a lot to me. I feel it says that I don't cut corners in either area of my profession. When you do cut corners, in my opinion, it presents something negative about you—that maybe you won't go that extra mile or will get lazy in the process. My dad was a person who always did things the right way, not redoing anything—he was precise and methodical in all that he did. I strive to be that way as well. However, in today's world you can get a clean, quality website for much much less.

Companies for Website Hosting

This is very inexpensive. Companies like GoDaddy can host your website content for around eight dollars or so as of this writing. They take care of keeping you online for clients to find. Other hosts you might take a look at include Web Hosting Hub, InMotion Hosting, and FatCow. Their prices may be even lower than the more well-known GoDaddy. Ask around and see what peers are using and how they like it. You can sign up for a multi year package to save time and money. Otherwise, you will get a yearly renewal notice.

So, overall, I would dedicate at a minimum about $1,000 for the website production process to be safe. Again, strive to find the best quality at the best price. You will most likely pay less than this amount, but remember, it will all add up later on if you go the cheaper route. For instance, if you start out with a basic pedestrian design, it will cost something, and then you will spend more later on to upgrade. In contrast, if you spend more now for a higher quality—be it for your demo or website—it is money you won't spend again. If you can swing it, go for the best now. Why delay your greatness?

Marketing: Your Name in Lights—or at Least on a Business Card

As I have said before, this is the voiceover business, not the voiceover charity. It is vital to have the right tools to keep your name out there in front of your prospective clients. These could include postcards, pens, pads, and business cards with your name, logo, and contact information. There are companies set up just to put your name on an item to promote you and your services. They call these companies *fulfillment companies.*

I suggest you enlist professionals in each area to perform their magic to promote your talents. This master technique allows you to get the genius of an experienced professional to work on your project. You can't go wrong there. It may cost a bit more, but I feel it is well worth it. My logo was done by a great graphic artist, and it gets used over and over. My business card was not, so now I want to have a new logo made for my teaching business. You want to present yourself as high-end talent, not as some patchwork quilt performer, using the cheapest, most expedient path you can. The most successful voiceover talent I have known have gotten quality promotional pieces executed by professionals and never looked back.

Union Membership

The Screen Actors Guild and AFTRA have finally merged. Please read the introduction from the SAG-AFTRA site:

> **The Most Distinguished Performer's Union in the World**
>
> SAG-AFTRA represents more than 160,000 actors, announcers, broadcasters, journalists, dancers, DJs, news writers, news editors, program hosts, puppeteers, recording artists, singers, stunt performers, voiceover artists and other media professionals. SAG-AFTRA members are the faces and voices that entertain and inform America and the world. With offices in Los Angeles, New York, and nationwide, SAG-AFTRA members work together to secure the strongest protections for media artists into the 21st century and beyond.
>
> **Giving You the Tools**
>
> In addition to negotiating and enforcing contracts for professional performers, SAG-AFTRA also offers members the tools to navigate the industry and expand their craft along the way. From the workshops of the SAG-AFTRA conservatory to resources for young actors, the Union protects and enhances member's quality of life on and off set, in the recording studio or working in the field covering a story.
>
> **Are You Ready to Compete as a Professional?**
>
> SAG-AFTRA membership is a significant rite of passage for every working professional in the media and entertainment

industry. (performer). However, don't be in a hurry to join unless you are sure that you're ready to compete as a professional. For actors, you should prepare yourself by studying, performing in plays and nonunion on-camera projects in order to build your resume and gain valuable experience.

When you are offered your first principal union job, we urge you to consider joining SAG-AFTRA, but understand it is a commitment. Need a disclaimer here that for broadcast members, joining SAG-AFTRA may be a requirement of accepting employment. Contact the National Broadcast Department or your nearest Local when you are offered a job in a SAG-AFTRA shop for more information and initiation fees.

Initiation Fee Loans Now Available for New Members

Eligible SAG-AFTRA performers are now eligible for low-interest rate initiation fee loans when joining the Union.

For example: On a loan amount of $3,099.00 with a fixed rate and 24 month term based on creditworthiness (including automatic payment discount), payment amounts will be:

$142.18 / month with 9.40% APR fixed (A Credit Rating)
$145.78 / month with 11.90% APR fixed (B Credit Rating)
$150.17 / month with 14.90% APR fixed (C Credit Rating A SAG-AFTRA)

Initiation Fee Loan is also available to current members who are assessed a difference of initiation fee. This may result when working in an area where the initiation fee is higher than the amount previously paid, as described on the back of the SAG-AFTRA Membership Application.

> Once you are a member, you must abide by the rules of membership, starting with Global Rule One and the No Contract/No Work Rule. And, whether you are a SAG-AFTRA member or not—never accept work during a Union strike!

As a beginner, you want to take work of any shape and size. Getting in front of a microphone and getting paid to talk is outstanding. At first, you will most likely be nonunion talent. This puts you in a pool with both inexperienced and experienced voiceover professionals but not the heavy hitters who work all the time or the celebrities. It's competitive but less so than union work. It should be much easier for you to land work as a nonunion actor than if you were in SAG-AFTRA.

After a while, however, you may be up for union spots. At that point you must decide whether you want to stay on the nonunion side of things or get ready to compete in the union arena. The union can provide the following:

- Session and residual income (money made for a run on the air of a commercial).
- Health and life insurance.
- Pension.

These are big advantages. Getting residual income is huge, allowing you to do other work while you make money with your commercials on the air. With nonunion work you get paid for your recording session, and then you get a buyout—a certain amount of money that covers all other use of the spot. For a newcomer this may suffice because you may think, "Hey, all I did was talk." But when you see the difference in a union run, you may not be so happy.

PART II: Up-Front Needs and Costs

SUMMARY

These are the most important needs and where you should spend your money:

- Quality coaching.
- A professional demo.
- A great microphone.

If you are well trained, sound great on your demo, and can record from home on a terrific-sounding microphone, you, my voiceover friend, are on your way.

PART III

Your Voice

Introduction

SECTIONS:

- Your default voice.
- Your voice register.
- Beginning voice types to master.
- The voiceover coach and how he or she will help you to improve.
- Breath.
- Voice techniques to correct mistakes.
- Techniques to alter your voice to get through copy more quickly and easily.
- How to maintain your voice for the rigors of the business.

The first question most beginners ask is whether they have the right voice for voiceovers. Most students feel like if they don't have a sexy, languid sound or a deep bass or one of those typical high-energy announcer-type voices, they are out of luck. This is not true on any level. The voiceover business welcomes all kinds of voices, from straight-ahead and clear to character types to raspy, sexy and smooth, nerdy, and rich and deep, to name a few. Each has its own place in the voiceover universe. You just have to find your niche and refine the use of your voice. Each of us starts with what I call a "default" voice.

The Default Voice

The default voice is the one you use every day in conversations, on the phone, and with friends and family. It is the one we fall into easily. It may be loud, it may be fast, or it may be very soft and soothing. It may be serious, or it may be witty and smart-alecky. No matter what the sound, it is the one we use the most in life.

Your default voice might be good for some voiceover needs, but it will most likely need to be refined and focused in for greater use in the business. It will have to be slowed down, quieted down, and often clipped to be cast for more voiceover work. You will frequently fall back into your default voice and have to be pulled out of it. You will speak too fast again, too slow again, or too loud again. It is up to the voiceover coach to train you to know when you are slipping back so you can do it yourself for audition and session work. You need to speak from other parts of your voice register.

Your Voice Register

The key in the voiceover business is not doing a wide array of funny voices but discovering and training the various parts of your speaking voice range. If you think of the middle as conversational, we can go up and down in many small increments to deliver reads usable for a variety of reads.

These areas should be mastered first:

- High energy.
- Conversational.
- Low, deep, and slow.

Example High-Energy Voices for Guys

- Local car dealer spots
- Phone service spots
- Fast-food spots
- Amusement park spots.
- Entertainment spots (e.g., Disney).

Example Conversational Voices for Guys

- Lottery spots (e.g., Illinois Lottery).
- Bank spots (e.g., Fifth Third Bank).
- Medical spots (e.g., health groups).
- Auto spots (e.g., Hyundai).

Example Low, Deep, and Slow Voices for Guys

- Beer spots (e.g., Dos Equis, Miller, etc.).
- Tourism spots (e.g., Illinois tourism).
- Lawn and garden spots (e.g., Toro).
- Construction spots (e.g., for work gloves).

Example High-Energy Voices for Women

- Retail spots (e.g., Sears, Kohl's, Target, etc.).
- Home product spots (e.g., SC Johnson products, including Off! and Oust as well as detergents).
- Restaurant spots (e.g., Applebee's).
- Theme park spots (e.g., Sea World).

Example Conversational Voices for Women

- Health care spots (e.g., hospitals, clinics, etc.).

- Nutritional spots (e.g., Yoplait yogurt, One A Day Women's vitamins, etc.).
- Grocery store spots (e.g., Cub Foods, Meijer, etc.).

Example Low, Deep, and Sexy Voices for Women

- Beauty product spots (e.g., Dove, face cream, etc.).
- Luxury car spots (e.g., Audi, Lexus, etc.).
- Vacation travel spots (e.g., Hawaii tourism, AirTran, etc.).

There may be different product categories not listed here, but this should give you a good start with understanding how these basic voices are used. Some categories might also require a different vocal sound than the one listed.

ULTIMATE VOICEOVER TIP!

Listen to commercials on the Internet, radio, and television and imitate them.

These voices are the winners in the casting process. Some, like quirky—nasal even—and upbeat and perky for women, are used again and again. You should listen and try to master these styles. As we will mention later, voice immersion is a big part of learning this business. We need to understand what sounds are most popular and make them part of our voice arsenal.

With practice, you will be able to provide a wide variety of different shades and sounds for auditions and sessions. You will take into account all the variables: fast, slow, high, low, and on and off the mike. You need to learn to speak from a variety of different spots in your voice register.

When I began, I prided myself on being the man of many voices, including dialects, impressions, and accents. I was great at high-energy stream-of-consciousness types of sounds. However, after a while, that style winnowed away, and I hit a bottom. What did I do from there?

Mindy Verson, a local casting agent in Chicago, explained to me that my lower, quieter register was a great place to speak from and that my voice had more of that quality than the voice-to-voice frenetic sound of my earlier reads. Now I had to learn to deliver my voice from that area.

In a short time, I was the national voice for Off! and Oldsmobile and the local voice for the Illinois Lottery and Harris Bank. In addition, I did a series of grocery store spots in a deadpan voice. Many times I would enter the studio to record full of energy and have to go down low to execute the spots given. It almost felt like I had trouble breathing when I was stifling all my energy. However, I learned to read from there, and I had my biggest years financially in the business. Thanks, Mindy!

So listen and learn. Establish your voice from different areas in your register, and you will be able to offer so much more as a voiceover artist.

The Voiceover Coach

A voiceover coach needs to take your special style of voice and teach it a few new tricks. If you are looking for coaching in Chicago, I will be happy to work with you. Other great coaches are Darren Stephens and Deb Doetzer, great VO talent that have the ability to help you improve with your reads and further your success. They can help with demo production as well.

One of my students, Scott, had a real Chicago salt-of-the-earth sound. It was good for some reads but not for most. I had to teach Scott to clip the end of his sentences for better speed and control of the copy. I lowered his voice a bit and got him to speed up on other copy. By the end of his demo with me, he had a whole new voice repertoire that arose from his own speaking voice.

Slowdown Technique

Do a slow and deliberate countdown from three before executing a read. Even if it feels like you are spinning like a top wanting to rush into your read, your brain will imitate this slowing down and help you deliver your copy point by point. Instead of shoving all the hors d'oeuvres in your mouth at once, sample, taste, and deliver each with intent. The countdown should go like this: three…(beat)…two…(beat)…one…(beat)…and then the read. The first line of your read has to be slow to introduce it anyway, so use this technique if you are lurching into copy.

ULTIMATE VOICEOVER TIP!

Use your copycat brain. Your brain loves to imitate.

We can get the brain to do our bidding by simply letting it do what it does best: imitate. If we set the tone, the brain will simply imitate the style of read you begin with. Conversely, the brain will imitate a mistake you create over and over again unless you slow down and correct it. So I suggest trigger your read with a piece of dialogue that sets the tone of your read. For instance…Say "Hey" to loosen up your read and make it more conversational. Say" Yeah, right" in a snarky way to flow into an attitude read. More later on in this book.

Light Read Technique

Many beginning students land on their words too heavily so that it sounds like they're really reading the words. Commercial copy is very informal for the most part. It has to sound realistically conversational and not read. Words get rounded off, and *t*'s become *d*'s, transforming *better* and *butter* into *bedder* and *budder.*

So try this technique: Underline the main points in your copy, including what the product does, how it works, where to get it, and so on. Then step away from the copy stand and speak extemporaneously about the subject as if giving a speech you rehearsed. See what you remember. Go back to the script if you need to remember a few things. Try again. Then go back to the script and read it. You should now speak more naturally because you know what you are going to say. This is how we speak in real life—with authority over what we are going to say. We don't usually communicate with someone unless there is something we understand we want to say.

Lower Volume Technique: "On the Cell Phone" Read

Maybe your voice is a little too hot and heavy for reading copy. It might just be too loud. Perhaps you have fond memories of having stories read to you by Mom or Dad or another loved one when you were a child. How loud were those read? Were they soft, soothing, quiet, and conversational or loud and raucous? Unless you had an unusual family, my guess is it was the former. So let's start there.

It all begins for me with the "on the cell phone" read. It used to be the "talk to the person on the barstool next to you" read, but now I prefer to call it the cell phone read. Use a calm, even volume and be to the point and natural. Hold up an imaginary cell phone and read your script into it or just begin an imaginary talk. "Hey, this is Jeff" I will be home soon. Just doing a voiceover session. Okay, talk to you soon." Nice and natural, no push. Shrug your shoulders and talk. This is where you should always start before reading any copy. You may need to adjust up or down from there, but essentially you are at the doorstep.

No matter how many techniques or problem-solving solutions I may throw at you, it all starts with one thing: your breath.

Technique to Kill the Accent or Regionalism

Some of my students read well but are hampered by a dialect or regional accent. This is not a reason to give up. I have discovered that the accent usually appears in the same place: at the ends of sentences. Certain words also display the accent more prominently. For instance, in New York, *dog* becomes *dawg*, and in Chicago, *Chicago* becomes *Chicahgo* (*cah* as in *cat*).

By identifying the problem words, you can circle them and eliminate their issues by inserting a new way to say the word. You can turn *dawg* into *dahg* and *Chicahgo* into *Chicawgo.*

ULTIMATE VOICEOVER TIP!

Clip the words at the ends of sentences while making a poking motion with your finger.

A good technique is to make a motion of poking the accented word like you would while popping a soap bubble. Say the word quickly while poking your finger. This will help you clip the word and prevent the accent from leaking out. This is good for any word you want to change in your script.

It All Starts with the Breath

If you are a singer, you know this to be true. But haven't you heard this in other parts of your life? When you are upset, someone says, "Breathe." If you are in a meditation, kickboxing, or yoga class, the breath is stressed for ultimate strength and control over what you are doing.

Doctor Al Sears developed an exercise regimen called PACE. It heavily involves increasing breath capacity, which helps your heart and other parts of the body maintain optimal health.

When breaking down copy into main points, it is essential to read each piece with strong breath control. If you are not present in each piece, your read will suffer because your brain will do what it is supposed to do: tell you to breathe.

Knowing that, you should never want to be at the end of a breath when reading copy. Why? Because you will have to reload on the next line, and that reading will be no good. What happens is that the first part of the next line is somewhat diminished with your gaining momentum again.

Your goal is to give your engineer and client usable pieces for construction. You need to stay present for each thought and avoid running out of breath, fading off, or reloading and jerking ahead with new energy that does not match what you just did a few lines before. This can be an editing nightmare! When you need more air, you disengage from the thought, and the line is useless. On playback, make sure you attack each line with emphasis and intent and avoid fading off due to lack of breath control.

ULTIMATE VOICEOVER TIP!

Begin and end each line with a full tank.

You never want your read to dip in energy when you are recording your copy. Work to complete each phrase or sentence with full energy and then reload and do the same for the rest. Think of them as quick martial-art punches, one after the other and each with strength. If you need to take a breath for longer copy, even if it adds a few seconds to the read. The engineer can cut out the dead space.

The following will happen if you don't do this:

- Your read will hollow out. It will get boring and detached in the middle.
- Your read will get an uneven energy or speed.

- Your read will get uneven volume.
- Your read won't edit well piece to piece.

The point here is to give good, solid pieces. Since all commercials are constructed and not completed in full takes, your job is to give them solid pieces, one after another, with full attention and strength. They will edit these together for the final spot or voiceover piece. When you search for breath, your mind disassociates, and this can be heard in your read. Remember, you are in front of a microphone that picks up everything, even when your mind wanders.

You may ask, "Can I take breaths in between copy points? Won't that be heard on the recording and sound funny?"

The answer is yes, you can take breaths. They will be edited out if they are too loud. With digital recording, anything is possible. If the sound of your breathing distracts you, remove your headset or move it to the back of your head and just speak. We will deal with exercises in this regard when we break down copy in part 3.

From here I will give you an idea on how to focus in your voice for maximum strength and efficiency.

Marking Up Your Copy

As I will mention repeatedly in this book, I want your process of reading to be stupidly easy. This counters the problems that can occur in sessions and at auditions:

- Nerves.
- Perfectionism.
- Competitiveness.
- Distraction.

One way to do that is by marking up your copy and breaking it down into smaller pieces to read one by one. Each piece read well adds up to a great spot. This takes the pressure off of you to read the entire script whole. This is not a monologue done for the stage. We just need to capture good piece by good piece. Imagine you get this script:

Your Bank

What does Your Bank have that other banks don't? How about free checking, even on the smallest accounts? That is what Your Bank has, even if your account balance is as low as ten dollars. How about no fees for overcharging for the first ten overcharges? That is what Your Bank does like no other. Plus you get a personal advisor to help you grow your money and show you ways to invest and increase your hard-earned income. That is Your Bank: there for you like no other. Why? because it is Your Bank. Come in and let us be Your Bank today.

Your normal approach might be to fly into this script, figuring that the more you read it, the better you'll get. This can happen, but you'll miss a lot along the way by not breaking it down to its essential components. Like a dancer learning a routine, each step carefully learned adds up to a precise routine. Now let's mark it up:

Your Bank

What does / Your Bank / have / that other banks / don't? / How about / <u>free checking,</u> /even on / <u>the smallest accounts</u>? That is what / Your Bank / has, / even if / your account balance / is as low / as ten dollars. / How about / no fees / for overcharging / for the first / <u>ten overcharges</u>? That is what / <u>Your Bank</u> does / like no other. / <u>Plus</u> you get a personal advisor / to help you / grow your money / and show you / ways to invest / and increase / your hard-earned/ income. / That is / <u>Your Bank</u>: there for you / like no other. / Why? / Because / it is / Your Bank. Come in / and lets us be / Your Bank / today.

Now when you read, just read each copy piece and keep flowing through the dialogue. Notice the underlined areas are where you put a bit more emphasis on the words and that some popular phrases like "grow your money" and "ways to invest" stay together to help you move through the copy faster.

Quick Tips on Reading Copy

- Start slow. Let the first line ground you into the pace and beat of the spot.
- Build speed as you go. Each line should be faster than the first.
- Decelerate as you get toward the end.

If you get into the spot slowly and grab the right pace, this can balance you through the rest of the piece so you don't lose the beat of the spot. This also anchors your breath so you can carefully measure out the right energy with each copy point you read. This makes you relax and gives you the ability to add more of your personality and nuance to the read. If you do this, you should have control over what you are reading.

I will talk more about this later in this book.

Voice Compression

While communicating, your voice's volume and range go up and down. It can be loud and soft. It can be higher pitched and lower pitched. If your voice was plotted on a graph, it might have many peaks and valleys. Imagine two lines cutting through this graph, one cutting off the top of the mountain and the other cutting off the lower part, parallel to the other line. You are left with the center sound of your voice, right in the middle, the meat of your voice, where it is strong, to the point, nice and focused. The sound is not loud but conversational and is easy to listen to over and over again. It carries the quality of your voice in its choicest, most usable form. That is what I want.

My job is to take the strength of your voice and compress it to make it stronger and more consistent. When I first explain this concept to my students, they feel they are going to lose something in this compression process. Then I point to an overhead light on the ceiling of our classroom. I say that if I focus that light into a laser, will the light be more powerful or less?

The answer, of course, is more. That is what I want to do with your voice. I take inventory of where the strength is—your most efficient high and most efficient low. Sometimes men have good higher and lower sounds; women obviously do. But what I want to do is keep the voice in the optimal area of both, never having it rise or fall into a zone that is not focused or not supported by breath.

Wherever your voice roams in conjunction with the copy, it has to be supported by breath and fully present. The tone of the copy will indicate whether it needs to be higher or lower on the register.

Exercise

Start low in your register and read the alphabet. With each letter, go up in your voice. Keep going and see when you feel your voice is starting to be strained. Now go down and see where it gets unsupported in the lower register. Now look to locate *the best lower note* and *the best higher note*. Practice just landing there automatically without doing the whole alphabet. This will enable you to understand your voice better and know how low or high you can go in a read. Keep doing the alphabet slowly to make sure you are present with breath for each letter.

If you do this, you will have taken inventory of your voice. This should give you a better idea of where it is supported by breath and where it is not. This voice should have a conversational tone like you would have if you were talking on a cell phone. There's no need to be loud ever. This is one of the first issues with untrained talent: they want to be louder than needed.

In life, you communicate in a basic conversational manner. You may incorporate different emotions into your voice but they are genuine, not forced or overacted. So why do that in front of the microphone? The same people you talk to in life are listening to TV and radio and don't want to hear you talk in a fake, loud, or insincere way. Novice voiceover talent thinks of the microphone as a place to get loud, like on a PA system at the local sports arena.

Practice reading from just that best lower note and then practice from just the best higher note. Eventually, move to a note one up or one down the register. The more comfortable you are with reading from these areas, the more you will have to offer when being directed.

It's like the old rabbit-ear TV antenna. You adjust to the left and then to the right until it's just right. By practicing, you will get used to delivering your voice from a consistent place and at a consistent level. Then you can move up or down and deliver it from there. This practice will help you in the studio when creatives want you to adjust. Practice at home in front of a microphone and get used to this process. This will make you look like a professional when you get the call to record.

ULTIMATE VOICEOVER TIP!

When reading into a microphone, think of it as your friend's ear.

You wouldn't yell into your friend's ear, so don't do it in front of the mike. Just talk as you do in regular life—in person or on the phone—with enough volume to be heard and the right emphasis or tone to be understood. That will work just fine.

OK. Next thought!

Once we become comfortable compressing our voice, getting to the center of our sound, we can deal with the time issues a commercial voiceover script presents.

Unlike with stage or TV and film work, your voice has a time limit in commercial work. You must get the message across in fifteen, twenty, thirty, or sixty seconds. But you will often end up with a script that is overwritten because it must cover all the client's copy points and legal clarifications so as not to be misleading in any way. You'll have a whole lot to say in very little time.

How to read copy fast

1. Read copy slowly and deliberately at first. Try this tongue twister: "Rubber baby buggy bumper." Say it slowly at first and then speed up until you are going quickly.

2. Compress your breath. Put your tongue behind your teeth. Make a "da da da da" sound. Take a breath and exhale your copy, shooting your words through a virtually closed mouth. This eliminates the big inhale and exhale that costs you time. Don't worry about volume. Conversational level is always best. Start there and adjust up or down slightly. Let your words rattle out by compressing your breath, squeezing it out so you can fly over the words quicker and easier.

3. Find phrases in the copy you can cluster together and read quickly. I'm going to give you a tag to practice on, but a few words before you start. The line breaks in this marked-up tag are to help you locate key phrases and focus on reading them one by one. Here it is:

> Financing example
> Forty-eight months
> $19.05 (read as *nineteen oh five*) per month
> Per thousand dollars
> Financed.

Now flow them all together: "Financing example, forty-eight months, $19.05 per month, per thousand dollars financed."

Return back to the entire script. Continue this pace for the rest of the script.

> Financing example, / forty-eight months, / $19.05 / per month, / per $1,000 / financed. / 25.9 percent / down payment. / Savings compare / 0.9%APR / to a banktown.com / national average / bank loan rate. Residency / restrictions / apply. You / must take / retail delivery / from participating / dealer stock / by July 18, 2011. Dealer financial participation may affect consumer cost. Not available with customer cash offers.

Remember, start slow and pick up pace. Take more time on words that don't flow easily, like *financing.*

4. Spell problem words phonetically for easier reading. Let's say you hit a problem word like *fortuitous.* When your eye hits it in the read, you may want to trip over it or stall a bit to grab it. If you want to follow my "stupidly easy" method of reading, simply spell it out in a way that says the word to you, such as *for two it us.*

Or perhaps the word is *arcade.* You would simply spell it out as *r kade* or *ar kayd*—whatever works for you. Write in pencil next to the word in big letters the spelling that makes it easy for you to read on the fly.

Make sure you can say each word easily. That will prevent unwanted pausing or tripping over words in the script.

ULTIMATE VOICEOVER TIP!

Mistakes mean slowdown.

When we make a mistake reading copy, the response can be anger, embarrassment, and often the need to speed up and say the mistaken line again quickly to cover up the mistake. I frequently tell my students to imagine a chair in front of an open doorway. If you tripped on the chair coming in, would you run through the door faster the next time and slam into the chair even harder? I would hope not.

The same is true with making a mistake. Slamming into the phrase faster gets you revved up instead of establishing a relaxed pace. It's a nice reflex to get into when reading copy: a mistake means slow-down. Go over the bobbled phrase or word slowly and then move faster. Remember, we learn everything in life slowly at first and then more quickly, so please don't disregard that fact in your read. Continue to go back to the "cell phone read"—this will remind you to slow it down, too.

Keep in mind that you will naturally read faster as you go. If you start with a slower read and speed up naturally, you will become more comfortable and more rooted in the read, and you will sound more natural. As a rule, you really don't need a lot of volume in most spots, so if you apply this compression practice right at the beginning of the spot, you won't go wrong. Then by lowering volume and using your breath efficiently, you will have defeated all time issues. This method works great for overwritten copy, quick dialogue, and tags the best. You can also use it to give your reads some speed diversity from line to line. Either way, voice compression rules.

ULTIMATE VOICEOVER TIP!

Record and review your reads.

When you start practicing, keep some of your early reads. Listen to them from time to time. You will begin to notice an improvement in things like speed and clarity. You should hear a more natural read that is less reminiscent of announcements and less phony. Being able to self-correct through listening to your takes being played back in-session, really makes you a professional. You will be less reliant on the client or producers to zone you in. The quicker you adjust, the quicker you will get to nuances in your read. These are little interpretations that add so much but can only be done once you have mastered the bulk of what you are reading.

What Kinds of Voices Get Hired the Most?

Listen to radio and television. What do you hear? Those are the sounds that are most popular. Somewhere in there, you should hear yourself. There are certain iconic or favorite sounds that seem to get hired over and over again. Earlier I gave you some simple places to start. Let's now go deeper and see the wide range of voice styles you need to master to compete well in the voiceover business.

Keep in mind that you have a signature sound to start with and from that you will fan out into others to see what your range can be. Remember the alphabet lesson from earlier. You have to establish the right breath control in the high and low parts of your voice. The more you know your own voice, the better. Here are some of the iconic sounds I hear currently as well as those I have heard over my many years in this business:

Men

- Straight and conversational—just being you.
- Straight, quiet, and conversational. Mellow.
- Straight and conversational with romance. Up on the mike (e.g., for food spots).
- For retail, a strong, driving sound.
- A newscaster's voice.
- A deep, dramatic announcer's voice.
- A deep, dramatic announcer's voice with comedic overtones.
- Nasally and wry-sounding.
- A fresh, young, friendly voice.
- A lazy dude's voice (e.g., for beer spots).
- A wise guy's voice with an attitude (e.g., a Denis Leary type).
- Deadpan.

Women

- Straight and conversational—just being you.
- Mom straight talk.
- Upbeat and friendly.
- Bubbly.
- Wry, friendly, and conversational (e.g., for home products).
- Sexy and quiet (e.g., for beauty products, high-end automobiles, etc.).
- A sassy party girl's voice with attitude.
- A newscaster's voice.

Where to Begin?

First, get used to focusing on the sound of your own voice. If you want to fool around with trick or animated sounds in between, that is OK, but the bulk of your time should be spent mastering the voices above and going up and down your register with consistency.

You don't have to grab them all at once. Try different copy with different styles of reads and see what works best. You will find that certain types of reads are natural for you and others difficult. Knock out the more natural ones first and then venture into the more difficult styles.

Where Do I Get Copy?

As mentioned earlier, watch different TV channels and the tape shows, commercials included. Then sit and listen and transcribe the spots to practice. Start a folder on your desktop called *Practice Scripts* and compile as you go. You can also find Internet sites like Edge Studio that have a wide array of scripts to download and practice. Either way, collect different styles of scripts and begin practicing.

But What if I Want to Do Great Character or Animation Voices?

Most of us baby boomers, especially guys, wanted to be the next Mel Blanc, going from one voice to the other. In my career, I have been able to do a lot of funny voices, and those can be seen on my loopytalk.com demo website. However, it became quickly apparent that I was going to have to learn to read using my own speaking voice to survive. But if you have a talent for funny voices, dialects, accents, and impressions, you can do a character demo track of a minute or more to showcase your wares.

Here is a master list of voices you should practice to compete:

Male Character Voices

Voices

Sports-loving guy with his buddies
Stuffy rich guy
Loving husband or boyfriend
Carnival barker
Auctioneer
Cowboy
Pirate/Parrot
Farmer
Surfer dude
Voice of God
Sports play-by-play announcer
Newscaster (in-studio)
On-the-street reporter
Interior monologue

Bogart-type detective

Dialects

New York
Boston
Minnesota
Chicago

Southern
Texan
Laidback Californian
ACCENTS:
Italian, Jamaican
Indian, Black
Irish Scottish, British, French.

Seasonal Sounds

Elves
Santa
Dracula
Boris Karloff
Vincent Price
Peter Lorre
Irish leprechaun

Video Game Voices

Soldier
Small and big voices (various applications)
General
Embittered, rebellious soldier
Gravelly guy
Evil villain (a light voice or a gravelly voice)
High-pitched guy
Wise man (Chinese…straight)
Dumb guy
Fearless warrior
Smart guy
Beasts (deep and mumbly)

Female Character Voices

Wife or girlfriend (light as well as hard-edged and sarcastic)
Young mom
Cute, bubbly girl or woman
Child (male or female)
Teen (male or female)
Sexy Sirens and femme fatales
Old woman
Stuffy rich woman
Crackly, cute voice; elf-like
Smoky voice
Southern belle
Marisa Tomei
Cousin Vinny (New York voice)
Witch
Gypsy fortune-teller

Newscaster
On-the-street reporter
Weatherwoman

Accents

British
Irish
Italian
French

Dialects

New York
Southern

Seasonal

Elves
Mrs. Santa Claus

Gaming

Soldier (serious)
Love interest of hero
Evil sorceress
Sexy woman
Strong warrior
Bossy wife
Smart wife
Police dispatcher
Cop

Thoughts on Getting Cast for Accents and Dialects

If a casting agent or agency is looking for an authentic accent or dialect, remember they have worldwide access to the real deal. If you are attempting, say, a British accent, unless it is a caricature voice used for animation or comedic purpose, you need to really study the nuances of the voice. The Internet is a great resource—particularly YouTube—to find out how to do legitimate accents. Immersion into the voice is vital to create an accent that is believable. Listen over and over and see what sticks. Ideally, download an accent to a recording device like an iPod and let it soak in.

ULTIMATE VOICEOVER TIP!
When learning a voice coupled with another, actively listen to the other one to learn the one you want.

What in God's name is Jeff talking about here? Many times I was given a voice sample to learn. Oftentimes, it had another character talking with my character. As I listened to my voice, I kept learning the other one instead. Why?

I thought about how I learned other voices in my day, from funny uncles to teachers to impressions of presidents and movie stars. I never actively listened and forced myself to learn them. They just slipped in as I was doing other things as well. So I applied this to learning voice samples. As I focused on the other voice, I found my voice slipped in more easily.. From there, I just repeated the process and learned the voice sample needed.

Voice Maintenance

As cliché as it may sound, your voice is your instrument, so take good care of it. In all seasons maintaining your voice is vital for being ready to deliver a quality read for an audition or voiceover session. Having struggled many times in my early years in this department, I learned what it took to perform at less than 100 percent and with the benefit of a healthy voice.

Monitoring Your Voice

As you read—especially for longer pieces like audiobook and video games—you must keep a close watch on how your voice feels. It's like when you try to draw a straight line without a ruler. The longer the line goes on, the more crooked it becomes. It looks all right for a while but not so much later.

Be mindful of the following:

- Voice dryness.
- Straining or voice catching.
- Coughing from using your voice the wrong way.

Once I was directing a video game that required the hired actor to do a police role. He got through some 1,500 lines in one day and returned the next day with a crashed, hoarse voice. Uh-oh. He was able to work by using the lower end of his voice, but his voice was out of gas for his final role. What could he have done differently?

- He could have talked as little as possible before his next recording.
- He could have put some nice hot water, lemon, and honey over his throat as a preventative.
- He could have kept hydrating during the initial recording.

Same as doing a vigorous workout after not exercising for a while, the body won't reveal itself to be sore until the next day or so, not during the action itself. So keep monitoring your voice, especially during a strenuous session of more than a few hours. If you do toast out your voice like this actor did, shut it down. Don't whisper—just be quiet and hydrate. Keep moist warm water soothing your vocal cords.

ULTIMATE VOICEOVER TIP!

Instead of coughing, pour water over your vocal cords.

When you feel the gunk collect in your throat, it is all too easy to just keep hacking and coughing to clear it. This just irritates your throat even more. Drink some warm (room temperature) water or apple juice. It's better to wash over the gunk than hack it out. It's not easy, but it is better for your throat.

Other voice tips include the following:

1. For tender throats, gargle with a mix of water and hydrogen peroxide.
2. Oil of oregano tablets help keep colds and flus at bay (research this online).
3. Shower test your voice for range. See how high and low you can go in your register.
4. Your voice will warm up in-session even if it sounds hacked at first.

Smoking and Yelling Prohibited

If you like to party or attend sporting events or concerts, your voice is going to get abused from yelling for your favorite athletes and copping a smoke outdoors with your buddies. The best answer to all this is to keep well hydrated so your voice can withstand the overuse. Buy bottled water to counteract the effects of alcohol. It is good to be conscious of what you are doing with your voice at concerts and sporting events. Be mindful that a raspy voice the next day could inhibit your range in front of the mike. When you get home, have some nice tea with honey and lemon and don't talk for a while—not even a whisper.

As far as smoking goes, for years VO talent used cigarettes to dry out their voices and make them sound deeper. Well, this is quite a price to pay for a signature sound. I used to let my voice just dry out naturally by not keeping it lubricated with water, and as this progressed, my voice got lower in sound.

I certainly can't tell you what to do, but staying away from cigarettes is always a good course of action.

Colds, Flus, Allergies, and Illnesses in General

Preventative care is your best bet. Being hyper vigilant in this regard really helps. But what does that require on your end? Certainly stay clear of those who have colds, flus, and other contagious illnesses. If someone sneezes in the car, open the window for some fresh air. At work, phones and shared keyboards should be cleaned periodically with wipes to keep germs at a minimum. Bottles of hand sanitizer have popped up all over workplaces. Avail yourself of this liquid, especially after handshakes with clients. Germs are most easily transmitted from hands through the ducts in the eyes, so do not rub your eyes with your hands if unwashed.

Get rest and eat right, especially soups and easy-to-digest and warming foods that don't tax the body. Exercise a bit. Sweat it out in a sauna or steam bath. You've heard this all before, and that is because it works.

I used to have issues with my throat and oftentimes went to a great acupuncturist. She really helped to clear up my issues, and I still use her whenever I feel something starting up. Again, just take great preventative care.

Colds and flus can wreak havoc on your voice and sinuses. Coughing can hack your voice, and the residue can end up lodging in your sinuses, giving you a stuffy sound. This is not fun. It takes a while for all that to clear out. Nasal sprays can help, but nice, hot steam at home will release the passages and keep everything moist.

In your home or apartment, the dryness of heating and cooling systems can do a number on your voice as well. Humidifiers and steamers help to add some moisture to the air. With forced air heating systems, dust blows out of vents and can cause nasal irritations. If you own your own home, get the ducts cleaned periodically. Have the cleaning company use a rotating brush so you can clean the sides as well. I kept a purifier next to my air vent in my bedroom and was amazed at how much dust was on the filter after the winter heating system. If you live in warmer climate markets, such as Los Angeles, air conditioning filters also should be cleaned periodically.

Ventilate your living area as much as possible. Open windows, let in fresh air especially after using cleaning fluids or vacuuming. Low end vacuum cleaners kick out dust that gets into your air in your apartment or home.

Allergies are even trickier. In the Midwest, mold is a biggie, and many have issues with it with the onset of the fall and all the leaves. Dust, pollen, animal dander, and other irritants can affect your voice.

With forced-air systems, keep your filters clean and keep the fan running at all times to ensure the air remains clean. Using personal air-filter canisters on your desk or near the heat vent also helps to keep these irritants to a minimum. I run mine in my office area all day long.
Rugs are also a culprit for air pollution inside. Use a vacuum with a great HEPA filter capacity to prevent dust and dirt from becoming airborne. Miele machines do quite a good job. Overall, the cleaner you keep your environment, the better chance you'll have of warding off germs coming down the pike. A lot goes into your voice's health; just be mindful of these tips.

On the Job: Tricks of the Trade

So maybe you're getting over a little something and your voice and nose are not up to snuff (pun intended). First off, you need to find out what capacity your voice does have to use that day. It might be a lower sound that is needed at the audition or recording session, so do the alphabet drill we talked about earlier to see where you are in the low range. Then do the same for the higher range; that is what gets compromised with illness. Do this in a nice, hot shower before the job. Bring a thermos of hot water with lemon and honey to lubricate your voice. Don't talk.

At the session, get in front of the mike and warm up. See what your voice sounds like after a few reads. Most times it will sound just fine. It's mind over matter. Don't tell the client you have just gotten over a cold or that your voice is not 100 percent. He or she might get alarmed and look for the diminished sound.

My trick was to say a quick hello, work on my script, and then get in front of the mike and work it out. Very rarely did I run into trouble. One time I had to do an Australian accent for a voice match where there was a line change in a spot I had recorded a few weeks earlier. My line did not match. I kept drinking my hot water and said a few prayers. Finally, it got there. The phlegm moved out, and I was able to match the sound. Another time I was just too stuffy, and they sent out for nasal spray. The problem was solved.

Homeopathy

You may use homeopathic drops or sprays if you don't trust traditional drugstore medicine. Be careful, however. Although they are diluted, I once used a bit too much on a narration recording and could barely get though a line without making a mistake. After sweating it out, I kept going and got through it. I cringed before listening to the playback, but guess what? It sounded just fine. I worked through it, not alarming the client or engineer.

If you really can't speak or are severely diminished, however, you have to be replaced. It is a shame, but you would otherwise cost the client extra, which can have long-standing repercussions.

Most times if you have taken care of your voice at the first sign of trouble, you should be able to get through a session. By compressing your voice and only doing the range you have that day, you can survive and live to fight another day. Just remember the old axiom: "An ounce of prevention is worth a pound of cure."

PART III: Your Voice

SUMMARY

We have learned a lot about your voice and how best to use it.

- ✓ We start with our "default voice," the one we use every day.
- ✓ We learned to read from different parts of our voice register.
- ✓ We know it all starts with the breath. Then it's all about staying strong through each copy point.
- ✓ We use voice compression to hit our voice's bull's-eye and also to pick up speed.
- ✓ We learned about the various voices that get cast.
- ✓ We learned how to take care of our voice and how to monitor its use.

PART IV
The Script

“It is harder than it looks and easier than you make it.”

—Professor Jeff

Introduction

Students experience an interesting paradox when they start looking at voiceover copy. Some may look at a script and think, “What’s the big deal? It just a bunch of words, prices, and dates. All I have to do is talk.” Others may say, “Wow, that’s a lot to say, and I have to have it all done in thirty seconds?”

As the first person learns the intricacies and individual sections of a script, he or she begins to say, “Wow, there’s way more to this than I thought.” The second person—after using my simple techniques to break down a script—will say, “I can do this now. This is not so hard”

They would be exactly correct on both accounts. In my ten-plus years of teaching, I have been struck by the fact that there are more elements to reading a script than I ever knew existed in the twenty previous years I had been interpreting voiceover copy. There are rhythms, speed changes, line differentiations, and voice fluctuations, and there is the necessity of breath control—all key components in a quality voiceover read.

The good news is you do all this every day already in your communications with others. You don't have to learn it but just identify what you are doing and put it before the microphone. I will help you do that in this section.

In my career I learned by doing—on the job and in the studio—making mistakes and developing positive habits to increase my business along the way. However, these positive habits stayed in my head, unlabeled and unprocessed in many ways until I began to teach. Like when revealing a secret recipe, I had to become more and more precise in directing my students to the quickest shortcuts to success. Many times it has to be a quick reaction or shift done under the pressure of the audition or session. There is no time to figure it all out.

I can remember not preparing a lot for my reads early on. I came from an improvisational background and thought I would just wing it in there and be in the moment. I thought I had more time than I did. The writers had many top voiceover talent in the waiting room and had to move them through quickly. When it was my turn, My audition would end too quickly because I did not have other choices to offer. Then leaving I would have the dreaded "elevator audition"—that great idea popping into my head now that I was more relaxed but no longer able to audition. So I changed my ways.

I began to prepare, marking up my script to make it "stupidly easy" to read. This relaxed me in the audition, giving me a clear road map of what to do. I also marked on my script other voice choices I might make, especially for character reads.

Sections

- Commercial Script Categories.
- Voice Immersion.
- Script Types.

- Script Metaphors.
- Preparing to Read.
- Your Script Checklist.
- Controlling Your Recording Space.
- Read the Specs.
- Marking Your Scripts.
- The Art of Voice Compression.
- Voice Triggers and Ramp-Ups.
- Statements versus Intimate Statements.
- Manual versus Automatic Reads.

Commercial Script Categories

The bulk of the scripts you receive for auditions will come in the following categories. Each one may have a slightly different or dramatically different approach. Keep in mind that you will be starting with a basic conversational or cell phone voice with each and then altering the style or sound of your voice to accommodate the type of script you are auditioning with. These are the typical categories:

- Alcohol (beer, wine, hard liquor).
- Retail (Walmart, Sears, Best Buy).
- Home products (cleaning supplies, laundry, repellants).
- Cars and trucks (car dealers, car companies, accessories including GPS and OnStar).
- Health care (hospitals, care providers).
- Insurance (home, auto, health).
- Food (restaurants, fast food, grocery items).
- Vacations (airlines, resorts, cruises, theme parks).
- Personal care (hair products, toothpaste, perfume).
- Sports (teams, events).
- Financial (banks, investment companies).
- Phones (cell phone providers, iPhone, BlackBerry).

- Entertainment (plasma TVs, stereos, DVDs, video games).
- Technology (computers, iPods, iPads).
- Education (local colleges, schools, programs).
- Self-improvement (weight loss, speed-reading).

So you can see that your voice could be of use for a wide variety of commercial copy. Listen and learn and then imitate in your own style. Some will be better suited for your voice than others, but give them a try as they come up in your auditions. Speaking of script types, it will serve you well to listen to the radio and television and notice the different vocal inflections that are needed for each. Before going further, let's take a moment to talk about the concept of voiceover immersion.

Voiceover Immersion

It is not just what we say but how we say it. Getting through copy cleanly and clearly is important, but how it should sound counts as well in the voiceover equation.

Like with any foreign language you choose to learn, you need to immerse yourself in the sounds and vocal styles present in the voiceover business. This is a big part of being a versatile voiceover performer. Many voices are simple sound files in your brain. The voices of fight announcers, auctioneers, and Gypsy fortune-tellers are all sounds you know already from the various forms of media you were exposed to early in your life.

Others you acquire over time. These include accents, dialects, and impersonations. For instance, recently I was auditioned for a *Godfather* voice for a slot machine.

Even as I was seeing *The Godfather* back in 1972 I was working on the nuances of the voice. From watching the film numerous times and practicing the rhythm of the voice, I can summon it up pretty fast. But what if you have never done a voice like this before?

Question: How do you learn how to do a certain style of voice?

I remember when I was learning how to play a blues harmonica in high school. I sat in my bedroom and listened to albums by the blues masters that featured a blues harmonica player—people like Paul Butterfield, Magic Dick, and Little Walter. At first I would play up and down the harmonica and try to simply match any note. Eventually I could hit a single note, then another, and then another. Finally, through repetition, I could begin to play along. After even more practice, I could do my own solo.

The same is true of the note of the voice. You may try to find a single sound that sounds like the voice you wish to imitate. In the case of an impression, you'll want to do the most common catchphrase like. In *The Godfather*, this would be "I'll make him an offer he can't refuse." Once I have done this, I find the rhythm of the voice and go slow at first before, through repetition, mastering the sound I could barely find days ago.

In review:

- Find a single note or phrase you can imitate.
- Find another and piece them together.
- Establish the rhythm of the voice.
- Start to add your own spin to your now-mastered voice.

Listen to recordings on other agency or personal VO websites and see what other voice actors are up to. YouTube is a great source of voice info as well. They sound a certain way, and if you master the sound or voice, you can win the audition faster because a clear match is all that is needed and most actors cannot produce these sounds easily. Work any angle you can. Also, keep up on trends. You need to know who is hot in show business and how that sound is asked for at audition time. The voices change like the wind, but you have to know who they are referring to come audition time. Keep that subscription to *People* magazine going.

I grew up in the 1960s and observed all kinds of voices on my radio and TV. I imitated them and mastered them. For instance, as a child we took the Hudson River train to New York to see movies in the city. The conductor would bark out the stops: "Next stop Ossining, Ossining next stop."

I imitated that sound, and little did I know I would use it years later for serious cash. I was doing a Coors spot for FCB Chicago, and they needed the sound of a New York train conductor. Well, all I did was open my mouth and shoot out the sound I had learned as a kid. The TV spot ran nationally, and I was well paid for my efforts as a young lad. Keep listening and playing around with sounds and voices. They could come in handy. They will increase your versatility and ability to get on the spot somewhere. Like with that old train on the Hudson River Line of my youth, you just have to get on board to enjoy the ride.

This is a powerful way to master the voice profession. Keep listening and keep learning how to use your voice, finding the flavors and colors that can give you more choices come audition time. You will be amazed at how many you can master with lots and lots of listening and, most of all, practice.

Script Types

In the voiceover business, you should be ready to read a variety of different types of scripts. Here are a few different styles you will come across:

- Commercial radio scripts.
- Commercial television scripts.
- Corporate and industrial reads.
- Narration.
- Audiobooks.

- Promos.
- Video games.
- Internet.
- Phone prompts.

Commercial Radio Scripts

I call these chatty scripts because they usually include a monologue or dialogue. They typically use this high-energy approach to grab the listener while he or she is driving or working at home or in the workplace. For the beginner, these may seem easier in that they are louder in volume than television commercials. Many of my students like radio spots because they get to be more active in front of the mike. Here are a couple of examples:

Monologue Style

Moneybags Instant Lottery: Thirty-Second Radio

(Specs: Upbeat energy. Excited by chance to win.)

Announcer:

Everyone could use a little extra money, and with Moneybags Instant Lottery, you could get it…instantly. Each day dozens of people win…people just like you! You could win ten dollars, twenty-five dollars, one hundred dollars, or up to one thousand dollars just from buying a one-dollar ticket. But you gotta buy a ticket to win.

Imagine a little extra money in your pocket. You might take a trip, go out for a fancy dinner, or just treat your favorite guy or gal to a movie. Moneybags Instant Lottery announces a new set of winners each day, so what are you waiting for?

Moneybags Instant Lottery…You could be a winner! Instantly!

Dialogue Style

Deli Blast: Thirty-Second Radio

Moe: Hey Joe, what you got there?

Joe: My new super-duper sandwich from Deli Blast.

Moe: Man, that thing is a monster.

Joe: No, I got the super-duper. The monster Deli Blast is eighteen inches.

Moe: Eighteen inches? That thing's gotta cost a fortune.

Joe: Not so, my friend. The super-duper is only $2.99, and the monster is just under five bucks.

Moe: Are you kidding me? Man, that thing is piled on high.

Joe: Yeah, delicious cold cuts and fresh veggies. They don't call it the super-duper for nothing.

Mary: Hey, guys. What are you up to?

Joe: I am showing Moe my super-duper.

Moe: And the monster is eighteen inches…

Mary: OK, guys, maybe you'd better get inside before somebody gets in trouble.

> Announcer: Deli Blast super-duper and monster sandwiches. In the sandwich world, size matters. Available at six convenient locations.

Radio scripts can use more wild concepts to keep the listener interested. If there is dialogue, you get to audition and record with multiple actors. This can be a lot of fun. The give-and-take with fellow voiceover actors improves your read by mixing your performing abilities with other talented individuals.

ULTIMATE VOICEOVER TIP!
When auditioning in a dialogue radio spot, stay focused on only your voice performance.

Being a team player, you may audition with someone and work together to do a great read. While the give-and-take may be good, spots are cast by individual voices, so you'll get no extra points for blending your voice with your partner's in the audition process. No matter how good your team is, it is very likely these three roles would be cast in three different cities. So pay attention to your character and don't be concerned with your partners. This may sound rude, but a struggling partner can pull you down by being distracting. It is up to each individual to bring a good character to the script, so keep your full attention on how you are sounding and don't get pulled into helping your partner if his or her choice is not as strong.

Commercial Television Scripts

Television commercials are quieter reads because audiences have a visual. As we observe the action on-screen, we don't need an announcer pounding us over the head with information. He or she gently points out what we are seeing and guides us through the commercial. I always call it a "don't wake the sleeping baby" read. When a new parent shows you his or her new child asleep in the crib, he or she talks over the crib but not loudly enough to disturb the child. Television commercials are the same way. A read gives us information about the product on-screen without intruding on the visual. Here are some examples:

Marcus Entertainment: Thirty-Second TV

(Shot of caveman watching insect crawl up a wall.)

Ann: Home entertainment sure has come a long way.

(Cut to shot of family in front of a big-screen TV with multiple screens.)

Now with the Marcus Entertainment three-pack, you can watch show after show all in a row. Literally on top of one another.

You get the ball game.

(Man gives thumbs-up.)

Your wife gets her dreamy doctor show.

(Woman blows a kiss into the camera.)

And Junior and his sis…They can fight it out for the rest.

(Kids wrestle with the remote.)

You can watch different shows on one screen in any room of the house. So you never miss a minute of action.

(Dad is getting a sandwich from the kitchen and catches a home-run. There are cheers as the sandwich flies in the air.)

The Marcus Entertainment three-pack…a three-ring circus of action all on one screen. Bringing peace to the American TV family.

(Family fights for the remote.)

At least, for a while.

Call Marcus today and get your three-pack. Call 1-800-MARCUS-3, and the fun starts today.

(Family looks at camera and stops fighting—and then resumes.)

Numbatrol: Arthritis Medicine: :30 TV

(Open on shot of grandma playing with her granddaughter.)

Woman (on-screen): I love spending time with my granddaughter. But some days, my arthritis pain flairs up, and I just can't do it.

(Shot of older man doing gardening.)

I'm still in good shape, but even a little digging here in the garden is hard when my arthritis acts up.

Ann: As we age, certain ailments can slow us down, robbing us of great time with family, friends, and activities we love. For painful arthritis, nothing soothes like Numbatrol.

Numbatrol goes to the site of painful arthritic pain, decreasing inflammation so you have more movement and, most importantly, no pain for up to twenty-four hours.

Woman: As my granddaughter grows up, I don't want to miss a precious minute. With Numbatrol, I won't.

Man: I love working with my hands. Thanks to Numbatrol I can get the job done…every time.

Ann: Ask your doctor about Numbatrol. Taken once a day, Numbatrol can give you the life you deserve, free of pain and discomfort due to arthritis pain. Numbatrol may not be for everyone. Possible side effects include dry mouth, bloating, and disorientation. Consult with your physician before taking Numbatrol.

(Shot of woman walking hand in hand with granddaughter to get ice cream. Man admires a new rose bush.)

Numbatrol for freedom from painful arthritic pain.

Audition Approaches: Radio versus TV Scripts

Obviously, the biggest difference between TV and radio is that TV spots have a visual. In addition, a quieter, more intimate voice is usually employed—think Jeff Bridges for Hyundai cars. Radio is brighter, chattier, and louder. More has to be covered simply by the voice.

For TV auditions, make sure you are conscious of what visual you are talking over. What are you playing against?

For radio, location is important to how you read. If you are in a dialogue, where does it take place? Is it quiet or noisy? As an announcer, clearly lay out the points you need to make one by one like a tour guide, carefully pointing out the details.

These vital points will give you a sharper, more focused read. Take some time and use your imagination. It could pay off big-time.

Animation Scripts

People like me got into the voiceover business to do this type of work. Creating original animation characters for commercials is a real thrill and lots of fun. Here are some basics on how to make interesting and fun animation voice choices:

1. Make a sound (e.g., singing, humming, talking, etc.)
2. Breathe in: make that sound again supported by your breath.
3. Talk through the sound.
4. Read different types of copy with this new sound (e.g., commercial copy, the newspaper, books, a cereal box, etc.).
5. Test-drive the character. Laugh, shout, whisper, speed up, and slow down.
6. Layer your voice: add an accent or gravel (lower your register).
7. Give your character a name.
8. Record and review your voice.
9. Make adjustments (look for where you exhibit poor breath control or your voice falls apart).
10. Record again.

Now try your newly minted animated character out on this script:

Character Cruise

Hey. I bet you've never met anyone like me. I'm (name), and guess what? I was just born, and I am ready to do some things. You know, commercials and movies. Stuff. I can laugh (laugh), scream (ahhhh), be real quiet (be real quiet), and just kinda hang… This concludes the character cruise. I'm (name). See ya later.

ULTIMATE VOICEOVER TIP!

In an audition or session, create contrast when being cast for multiple voices.

In an audition or session, you may have to do multiple characters. Don't get chatty with your fellow performers. Plot your move for each character. Create contrast. Do high and low, fast and slow, dumb and smart, in on the mike and off of the mike, raspy and clear, or young and old. You have to move fast when you get in there. Even if you are not being asked to do both auditions, prepare for both. Create contrast with your partners. If your voice blends with auditioning partner, neither of you will benefit.

For the below script,
Try Bee #1 as smart using a quick dialogue style.
Try Bee #2 as dumb with slow, ponderous dialogue. First try each voice individually and then try both together, back and forth.

Character Script: Two Bees

> Bee #1: Party time! Looks like the Smellingers are having a bit of a shindig.
>
> Bee #2: Mmm. Barbecue chicken. And potato salad. Let's get down there.
>
> Bee #1: We gotta hear from Jerry. He's casing out the joint. Says they have this new bee umbrella thing.
>
> Bee #2: Bee umbrella? What's that?

Bee #1: It's this lamp zapper thing that protects people like the Smellingers from bees like us.

Bee #2: Why does somebody always have to ruin our fun?

Bee #1: Once it goes on, we move off or else—

Bee #2: You mean?

Bee #1: Curtains…

Bee #2: What a world. An honest bee can't even buzz a bucket of barbecue anymore.

Bee Jerry: This is Jerry checking in. Bee umbrella in place. Cancel all flights. I repeat, cancel all flights.

Bee #2: Now what?

Bee #1: I hear there's an open Coke can at the park?

Bee #2: Probably hot.

Bee #1: You got something better?

Bee #2: Let's go. Boy, a bee's life can be such a disappointment.

Bee #1: Ain't it the truth, ain't it the truth.

If you want to try accents and dialogues with this voice, go for it. Just make sure there is contrast at all times.

ULTIMATE VOICEOVER TIP!

Use your trigger sound to get back into character or create new characters.

Once you have created your new character by speaking through a single vocal sound, you don't want to forget it. So keep in mind what trigger sound you used so you can simply fall into the character again and not have to search for it or recreate it. Also, when you need to create a new character on the spot, go back to the method above and create yet another new character for yourself. This is your key through the door. Once you are in, you will know what to do and where to go.

Try each character with a different voice. Come up with two distinct trigger sounds as described above. Easy places for variety will be fast-slow, loud-soft, dumb-smart, gravelly-light, etc.

Narration

Narration scripts require long-form reading as they tell stories that take longer than short thirty- or sixty-second television spots. They can be for broadcast on your cable station, such as Ken Burn's *Baseball* show on PBS or an interesting show on the dangerous lives of loggers on the Discovery Channel. They can also be for nonbroadcast use for corporate clients, telling the long and storied history of a company for the annual sales meeting or introducing a new product for the sales force. With narration, you have to be more precise in your read and establish a tone that will last ten, twenty, thirty, or sixty minutes or more. Here are a few examples:

Austin (caring and concerned)

On the far West Side of Chicago is the Austin neighborhood. It's a place where the arts are transforming lives. Where dance is lifting people to greater heights. Where self-expression leads to self-respect The Austin neighborhood is a special place where the arts give its people a chance to express themselves and be heard. A place where we stand up together!

Russell Stover (upbeat and smiling)

Russell Stover is the third-largest manufacturer of chocolates in the United States. They produce nearly one hundred million pounds of chocolate a year. It's always been a smooth, sweet, creamy affair, and no has done it better since 1923.

Medical Mombo (businesslike)

Welcome to Anatomy and Pathophysiology for ICD-10-CM. Today we will discuss blood disorders. An increase in the normal number of leukocytes is called leukocytosis, while a decrease in this number is known as leukopenia. They are all produced and derived from the hematopoietic stem cell in the bone marrow. We will discuss this more later in the webinar.

Hobby Shop (friendly)

Having a hobby is important in life. It takes away stress and engages you in a way that brings out the real you. There are all different types, and you can get started anytime, no matter what age you are or where you are in life. A hobby can bring you together with others of like minds, creating social situations from the enjoyment of a shared passion.

Tour Narration (friendly and conversational)

To many of us, history is something that happened somewhere else, in a different place and time. Here in Miami, history is alive right in our own backyard. Whether you are a Native American, a native south Floridian, or merely a visitor, the Miami Circle is our history, and this history keeps getting more exciting with each passing year.

From the glittering high-rises to the speeding boats in Biscayne Bay, we have something to keep you entertained and wanting to come back again and again.

Serious Narration

In countless emergencies every day, risk assessment, deployment of resources, and real-time command and control are critical to protecting lives and property. Honeywell's T-Hawk Mav is an unmanned micro air vehicle that provides situational awareness for all types of government security. Let me show you how.

These are not complete scripts but samples of longer works. Each one has a different tone and different challenges—some of the terms used in the Medical Mombo script are especially difficult. As we move through this section, I will give you tips on how to handle each one of these unique scripts.

Audition Approaches: Narration

Some initial research of words and terms may be required. Certain medical terms and disease names can be looked up online to find the correct pronunciation. M-W.com, the Merriam-Webster site, has audio clips of many of the terms you may need help with learning.

Since narration is long form, you need to establish a rhythm with your voice that stays consistent throughout.

ULTIMATE VOICEOVER TIP!

When reading narration copy, redo the first page after you have done the entire script.

The first page has a high level of trial and error to it. You get your flow by page two or so. After you do the last page, keep going and do the first page again. This way it gets the flow treatment as well and the read will sound more uniform overall.

Audiobooks

Reading for audiobooks has become a booming business. Audiobooks are the longest form of reading you will do—you may read up to a hundred or more pages in a single day. This can really tax the voice, and the reading style has to be consistent for it to work. It has its own set of challenging requirements:

- Read book multiple times to understand.
- Establish different voices for different characters and apply them consistently.
- Keep your voice lubricated with fluids while reading.
- Research proper pronunciations of people, places, and terms in book beforehand.
- Read for many hours at a time.

There are many book types you could read, including novels, nonfiction, spiritual works, technical works, and more.

> **The Mystery of Drood Street**
>
> The fog rolled in, blanketing Drood Street with an impenetrable mist that evoked play and terror. For the child, the translucent cloud would make for an excellent game of hide-and-seek. For the knowing adult, jaded by loss and unrelenting violence, the fog represented menace, unyielding and foreboding.

> Deiver: I hate this stuff. People get funny. Drive with their brights on. Blind you when you just want to get home. It just springs up like some weird jack-in-the-box. Scares me when this happens—I just want to go home and shut the door tight.
>
> Marco: Ah, what are you afraid of? Bad stuff happens all the time, even in broad daylight. Hell, you and me played in this stuff on Halloween, remember? Down by Parson's Creek? Couldn't get enough.
>
> Deiver: Same night Joey died in that creek.
>
> Marco: He was stupid. Never should have gone down there in the dark. That kid was a little slow anyway.
>
> Sally: Deiver? Deiver? Are you out there?

Read this story excerpt using a different voice for the narrator, Deiver, Sally, and Marco. Read in and out of the voices to gain consistency.

Promo

Promo scripts are exactly that: scripts that promote a show, movie, or program. They have a certain style that is upbeat and almost exaggerated. Talk shows have a signature sound that is very "announcery" although pushed a bit further. They overplay the dialogue to grab your interest.

Many times for commercial reads, they will say they want a "nonannouncery" read. Here is a chance to be an announcer and not hide your head in shame. Ha-ha.

The Ellen DeGeneres Show: Thirty-Second Promo

Announcer: On the next Ellen…

What happens if you want to be a dancer but you really can't dance? Dance expert Marie Legard shows that even if you have two left feet, you can still dance like a pro.

Then, comedian Jackie Mason tells tales from his new autobiography, *Oi, Do I Have a Story for You.*

Actor and writer Steve Martin performs on his banjo.

Comedic lawyer Ellen Friedman shares crazy divorce stories.

The fun starts here every day at two o'clock.

Dead Man Talking: Thirty-Second Promo

Ossining is a small town on the Hudson River.

In 1955, it was the site of one of the most memorable executions in crime history: the death of Whitey Lipman.

Lipman killed five people in a wild murder spree—and paid the ultimate price: electrocution…or did he?

People from the town think Whitey didn't die that day. That he still may be alive. That the man they think murdered five people in cold blood is this man: popular news anchor…Claude Lepass.

Is this just another Ossining urban myth…or is Whitey…a dead man talking?

Dead Man Talking. Coming to theaters this summer.

Video Game

For video games, you will get character breakdowns and a description of your character and his or her lines in the game. The lines may not be sequential, so you have to understand what is happening in the scene as you audition for the part. Take a little extra time here to prepare.

ULTIMATE VOICEOVER TIP!

Talk from the character's hologram.

"What in the heck does that mean?" you are probably saying to yourself. "Jeff has really gone off the deep end now." Well, hold on. Here is what I mean. Place the character you are doing in an environment. If he or she is about to be killed, see the gun pointed at you, the darkness, and the dank alley you are in. Take it all in before you speak. As I communicate about anything, I am usually reacting to something. Let that be your motivator. Where the character is and what his surroundings are…dare I say…"talk from the character's hologram."

Video Game Characters

Roughneck:

Mid thirties to late forties.
Street-smart, low-level mob enforcer. Loyal to the boss. Has violent tendencies.
Speaks with a New York accent.
Confident and wisecracking.

Please read all parts.

(Two roughnecks greet their boss.)

Roughneck:

Hey, Vinnie. Check out the rack on the brunette to your right.

(Their boss looks left.)

Roughneck:
No, no…Your other right.

(The wise guy and his crew engage a large group of enemies.)

Roughneck:
You pieces of shit, you're dead, you hear me?
I don't care who you guys are.
You're dead!
Who the hell are these guys?
Who the hell do you think you are?

(Two Roughnecks discuss their boss's sanity.)

Roughneck 1:
I dunno. It just don't seem right. I think the guy's friggin' nuts.

Roughneck 2:
You think the boss is a nut job?

Roughneck 1:
What, you don't?

(Their boss appears out of nowhere.)

Roughneck 1:
(nervous)
Oh, hey, Joey—lookin' good, Boss.

Again, this is just a sample of a game so you can get a feel for the characters. Remember this when reading characters:

ULTIMATE VOICEOVER TIP!
When practicing your part, do all the lines as your character.

Many times you will get a character who may not have a lot of lines. So rather than working on just the few lines you have, read all the lines as your character. This warms up your character so that when you return to your few lines, you will sound authentic.

Don't overdo the voice, especially if a lot of yelling is involved. Gaming voices can be very taxing, so save the full read for the recording. Also, keep hydrated and soothe your voice with tea with honey if need be. Lower your volume while practicing to save your voice till you are in front of the mike recording the actual material.

Creeper

Slight British accent. Raunchy, imp-like character. Dupe of his criminal boss. Characteristics: Mischievous, ruthless, sarcastic.

Creeper:
'Ello, monkey. Sorry, love. Ain't no shower in your noodle. (Laughs.) Let's play. C'mon. Places to go and people to kill.

(Creeper reacts to being electrocuted.)

Ha-ha. Is that all ya got, mate? Haven't felt that good since the Dark Ages.

Remember to set yourself in the hologram of the character. Where is he coming from when he speaks? This is very important stuff when it comes to creating your character.

Internet Content

Internet content is a great place to start for beginning voiceover talent. Many times a client will have a website and need some basic narration done to handle the explanation of his or her services. For the beginning voiceover talent, this can be a less pressured and less competitive opportunity to learn your craft. It is not as highly visible as radio and television work and therefore not as client managed.

Doing Internet work can get you the valuable experience you need for bigger, more high-profile work. You can expect less takes till completion and less client interference. If you have a connection with the creative team hiring, you can be an easy choice to do the work. On more high-profile radio and television work, the need for a "name" or celebrity talent might eliminate you from the competition. Also, the audition process will be less fierce due to the smaller scale of the work.

The work itself can be high quality and useful, providing you with a link to hand out to show off your voice. It is a great place to start and also a great place for experienced talent to show off their vocal prowess.

> **Cupcake Heaven**
>
> What is a cupcake really, a piece of heaven? A delightful dessert that makes you smile with each bite? Well, at Cupcake Heaven our cupcakes are beyond delicious. They are…well, heavenly. What makes a Cupcake Heaven cupcake so good?

This is a simple piece of dialogue to sell the website. There won't necessarily be a mass audition for this, and if you have the right style of voice, you stand a good chance of landing this type of spot.

> **Hotels.com**
>
> You have a smartphone. You use it all the time. But did you know your smartphone can be even smarter? Especially when it is used to find that perfect hotel on Hotels.com.
>
> Just hit the app button, and you'll be ready to take a trip around the globe for the most glamorous—or the least expensive—hotel on the planet. All on your smartphone.

This internet content may be accompanied by a basic piece of animation that your voice will be plugged into. You may be given a link to watch the animation before recording your audition. This way you can get a feel for the Internet piece, its pace, and the general style.

Your read will most likely be a bit underplayed and not loud or over-the-top in delivery. Remember you are just there to help move the information and the visual along. Your voice should not get in the way of the copy or flow of the spot.

Phone Prompt

When I got into the voiceover business, I wanted to do funny and zany voices. I did get to do a lot of them, including iconic ones like the little Raid bugs for Raid bug killer. I also got to sing the Good 'N Plenty song from my youth and many more. However, the voiceover business is a business of reading scripts and interpreting words no matter what they are and no matter whether they are funny or not. You will find that most of the work is conservative, regular, conversational copy that doesn't require us to man the mascot outfit and hide out in a voice.

No, our regular speaking voice will do the trick. Surprised? Well, don't be for long. A lot of work goes into just sounding like yourself and speaking with intent and purpose. Phone prompts require just that.

These are the messages we get from services and businesses that prompt us as to what steps should be taken to get our questions answered and our needs met.

> **Jamworld**
>
> Thanks for calling Jamworld, the number one location for all your party goods and equipment. If you are planning a party and need some help, please press *one*.
>
> If you are checking on rental equipment for your party, please press *two*.
>
> If you need a reorder of party goods and materials, please press *three*.

There is nothing glamorous about phone prompt voiceover; however, it pays real money and could be a steady gig for you when you are starting out or are in the middle of your career. Many spots are onetime affairs, but phone prompt work could bring in a steady income that can keep you going in between commercials. That is the beauty of the voiceover business: there are so many ways to use your voice and get paid for it.

Before we begin performing the script, let's lay the groundwork with a couple of my favorite metaphors about the technique of reading a script.

Script Metaphors: The Script Like a Dance Routine

It occurred to me that learning an entire script is a lot like learning a whole dance routine all at once. If you were to learn a hip new dance routine, your process would be to learn it one step at a time and then incorporate each step gradually. You would not be expected to hit the stage having mastered all of it at once. The same applies to your script.

Doing a good read of a thirty- or sixty-second script from top to bottom requires you to break down each part or dance step into individual components. You should then master each one, practicing the parts or pieces of the script that differ in tone and intensity, and then, once you are comfortable, you should be able to put all the pieces back together and read it capably and comfortably as a whole.

Looking at a whole page of words can be a daunting task for a newcomer—it's like looking at each step of a marathon run. However, when you break down the script to its essential components and read them one by one, knowing that you can do pickups to get the words you missed, you will have a more relaxed and easy go of it.

Again, make things stupidly easy for yourself and you will bring down the house!

Preparing to Read

Before reading a script, it is important to get prepared. That means doing the following:

- **Taking control of your recording space.** We mentioned in the first section that placing your script on the copy stand and asking for a proper volume level and microphone level puts you in control. Even though you are being directed, the more focus you put on what you are doing, the less you will obsess over pleasing the client. Do your job right, and all will be well. Asking the engineer to adjust your microphone to the proper height for you may be the first thing you ask. This starts to put you in control of your recording space. Studio microphones are very, very expensive. A talent could easily damage a mike by moving it around. So leave the adjusting to the engineer on duty. It is just the way to go.

- **Taking control of your script.** Notice how I keep mentioning control. I don't want you to be a control freak—just someone who can adeptly and easily handle each step in the process of reading a script. The object is to make the script your own. In this section, I will give you some easy-to-learn steps to master your script. If you perform them again and again, you won't get lost in all the words or in your expectation level of yourself. Speaking of expectations, check out the next section. I will discuss a concept I use with my students to get them thinking of getting to work rather than trying to be perfect.

The Brick Wall versus the Bull's-Eye: Building the Perfect Read by Being Imperfect

Many times as a voiceover actor, you will want to perform the perfect read. You may be in a good mood. Perhaps you had a delicious breakfast and you feel like you're going to nail it. You read the script and then take the arrow out of your quiver and fire at the target when you hear the words "take one." Then perhaps you do nail it on the first read.

But then you have to read it again because the first take or two is for the engineer to get his levels, and now he is ready to capture your reading magic—only the magic seems to be gone. "Take three." You shoot at the target, and your arrow this time hits a tree in the woods. "Take Four!" This time you hit an unsuspecting animal in the backside. "Take ten?" Uh-oh. Maybe that breakfast wasn't so good after all.

It's a lot of pressure to be perfect—to start in silence and hear the engineer say "take one" and nail it perfectly time and time again. So let's make it stupidly easy: look at your audition or recording session as building a brick wall and leave the archery to the archers.

Perfection time is over. Let's roll up our sleeves and get to work.

In the brick wall method, you first get your materials. That would be you, the talent, and of course, your script. The script is full of words. These are your bricks. Next, you mark up the script, which means laying out the design of the wall. Once you have the bricks, the words, and the design, then it's about how you, as an actor, are going to build the spot itself.

Give a leisurely, slow read. Remember the first take or two is for you and the engineer to get in sync—again, there is no need to hit the bull's-eye because even if you did, the creatives are not going to use the first take or two. Work it and start to build the wall. You speak clearly and in the right tone and now at the right speed. You botch a word. No problem. That word or brick is taken out and a new one put in. Keep building.

After reading word after word and placing brick after brick, you will soon find that—voilà!—the wall has been built and the script completed. You have given them full takes, good pickups, and great bricks that hold the spot together. The creatives love you, the clients love you, and guess what? You have hit the bull's-eye after all! Nice job. Go out for a great lunch. You deserve it.

ULTIMATE VOICEOVER TIP!

All commercials are constructed rather than done in one take.

In a voiceover session, you will do complete reads and then pickups—pieces of the script. From there, the creative team will construct the best of what you said and make a commercial. Knowing that, your job is to give them good solid pieces to use, not masterpiece full reads. So mistakes are allowed. Prepare, read your script, and then correct errors and read again. Let them direct you to the next thing, and all will be well.

A lot goes into reading a script well. Prepare yourself to do the same actions each time and you will find your reads to be easy. The following checklist contains what I feel are the essentials to approaching your scripts with creative consistency. This will make your job...What do you think I'm going to say? That's right: stupidly easy to do.

Step One of Script Reading: Break It Down

a. **Read** the specs of the spot using the reading style needed.
b. **Say** the product or service being sold and then read it slowly each time in the script.
c. **Mark up** the script to put it into manageable bites.
d. **Locate** difficult words and sentence structure, read slowly for proper pronunciation, and then break up run-on sentences for easier reading.
e. **Practice** repeat words found in the script.
f. **Cold read** to check markings and get a feel of the script overall.
g. **Revise** markings, discovering new rough patches and then revising again.
h. **Write** the point of the script in one simple sentence on top of the page (e.g., "Sears is having a great sale," "Get a better night's sleep with Serta," etc.)

Let's try this out with the following script:

AirTran Airways: Thirty-Second Radio

Wouldn't you love to relax in a tropical desert island, someplace far away but not so far from home? Introducing saver fares from Air Tran Airways with special flights to Silky Water Resort on Grand Bahama Island any time you want them.

With saver fares you get the price you need when you want to go. Saver fares from AirTran take you to the Bahamas for only ninety-nine dollars, to Jamaica for one hundred and nine dollars, and to Grand Cayman Island for one hundred and twenty-five dollars each way.

Plus you can go to Silky Water Resort on Grand Bahama Island for less than two hundred and seventy-five dollars round-trip.

Call 1-800-AIRTRAN for reservations. Saver fares from AirTran: the only way to fly.

A. Read the Specs of the Spot

The specs attempt to describe "the voice in the writer's head." They are at the top of the script or on a casting sheet describing the role you will play. Sometimes the description is longer than the role you play. It doesn't matter. The writer is just trying to zone you in. Here is where you get the litany of descriptions like the following:

- "Easygoing and conversational."
- "Upbeat, friendly, and conversational."
- "Sexy and playful."
- "Regular guy. Not announcery."
- "Authoritative read."
- "Overdramatic, big voice. Voice of God."
- "Wry. Hint of sarcasm."
- "Deadpan. Emotionless read."

Each of these describes a particular voice style. Sometimes the writer will mention a flavor-of-the-month actor or actress to indicate the style they want. Perhaps it will be a vintage actor for niche roles, like Vincent Price for a scary Halloween spot or Marilyn Monroe for a sexy, playful sound. Note, however, that the voice style they give you is just a reference; you don't need to do a perfect rip or impression of the voice. A common mistake early on is trying to impersonate the voice in the spec for the spot.

ULTIMATE VOICEOVER TIP!

Lets hear you!

When reading your specs for a spot, you don't have to do a perfect impersonation or rip of the style given—just your take on it in your fun and unique style.

The writer may ask for a style similar to a current VO style—say, Sam Elliott for a tough Western-sounding style or maybe Glinda the Good Witch for a fairy style. They don't need it to be spot-on—just in the spirit. They want to hear your voice coming through that style. That is what makes it fun and unique. Have fun with it. You don't have to be perfect.

B. Say the Product

Maybe your product is saver fares from AirTran Airways. Say it three times for starters: "saver fares from AirTran Airways, saver fares from AirTran Airways, saver fares from AirTran Airways."

Make sure you pronounce AirTran in a way that gives *Air* and *Tran* equal emphasis. Say the product or service name slowly at first and then faster. Remember, you are supposed to be the expert, so any hesitation in saying the client's name will make it sound like you don't know what you're talking about. The key to sounding confident in what you say is being able to say it with ease.

C. Mark Up Your Script

Marking up your script is crucial to establishing that brick wall theme. You want to read one copy point after another and not worry about what is next or what came before. Flow through the piece in front of you.

This is your road map—your GPS system—to get you where you need to go. Marking up the script breaks down a page full of words into small pieces of information to deliver in the style needed.

By breaking the script down from an entire performance to mini line readings, you can focus better and be more present to each line or phrase.

So here is what to look for when marking up your script. Some of this information may overlap with what we said earlier, but that is OK. It is important to impregnate this into your mind-set when you read your copy.

- **First,** underline the name of the product or your client's name. It may be Southwest Airlines, Morty's Pizza, or Dove Replenishing Bar. Say the name numerous times to get familiar with what you are selling. Since you are the spokesperson for the product, you need to sound well versed while saying its name. This is the "fake it till you make it" plan. If you say it over and over, it will sound like you know what you are saying and speaking with authority. This is particularly important when doing narration scripts with difficult medical terms or doctors' names. If you stumble or pause for even a nanosecond, it will sound like you don't know this person, product, or medical procedure. You want to build this muscle stronger than the rest of the script because that is what you are selling or presenting to the listener. Take extra time to get the pronunciation correct so you sound like the expert. If there is a word you don't know, you can consult M-W.com for dictionary audio pronunciations.

- **Second,** locate difficult words and sentences and cut them down to size. Run-on sentences, difficult terms (like medical terms), and the like can derail your read. Circle them and cut them down to size to read easier. Pay special attention to breath spots in these conditions. Take this, for example:

> Graymore Hospitals offer the most comprehensive health care for seniors, specializing in octogenarian care and neuromuscular disorders at their three central Chicago locations.

In this case, consider *octogenarian* and *neuromuscular.* Say each one slowly: *octo...gen...arian* and *neuro...muscular.* Then speed up.

Next, cut up the sentence in general, like so:

> Graymore Hospitals / offer / the most / comprehensive / health care / for seniors, / specializing in / octogenarian / care / and / neuromuscular / disorders / at their / three / central Chicago / locations.

- **Third,** separate groups of words you can say easily as one thought or in one breath. I call these *cluster nouns.* Cluster nouns are multiword phrases that we say easily in one quick burst. Usually, they are phrases we are familiar with in life. For instance:

    - In a million years.
    - Goes to work.
    - Cleans them away.
    - Forever and a day.
    - A part of life.

Picture the script like an old math test. It is best to do the easiest problems first and then the next easiest and so on until you reach the real mind-benders. The same is true of scripts. Do client names and cluster nouns first and then go from there.

- **Fourth,** underline all nouns, adjectives, and active verbs. These would include words like the following:

    - Food stains.
    - Airline.
    - Convertible.
    - Meaty.
    - Delicious.
    - Simple.
    - Growing.
    - Spills.
    - Cleans.

Let's look at some scripts that apply the techniques just mentioned. I have marked some up for you to get you started and then left some clean scripts for you to practice. Consider the following:

Sample Script: Unmarked

Need a relaxing vacation? East-West Airlines flies to all the great cities you want to explore. How about a quick weekend getaway to New York City or a nice spa trip to Colorado Springs? We take you there at a price that will have you packing your bags…now.

Sample Script: Marked

Need / a relaxing vacation? East-West Airlines / flies / to all / the great cities /you want to explore. / How about / a quick weekend getaway / to New York City / or / a nice spa trip / to Colorado Springs? We / take you there / at a price / that will have you / packing your bags / …now.

This is the way it works best for me. Feel free to develop your own style, but chopping the script down to size makes it much easier to handle and, of course, read.

Now let's take a look at some more sample scripts and how to mark them up. Here is a spot as you would receive it, unmarked:

Home Product: Ready Stain Remover

Announcer:

Stains. They're a part of life. Food stains on your favorite shirt. Grass stains from wrestling with the kids. Grease stains from changing the oil in your car. Stains may be here to stay, but now you can clean them away with Ready Stain Remover.

Ready Stain Remover contains special scientifically engineered enzymes that react with your stain to break it up and remove it with a simple wash. Just apply when you spill, rub, or grind something onto your clothes. Ready goes to work in seconds.

The stain starts to fade and after washing, disappears altogether. And Ready is not allergenic, so it's safe to put even on baby's diapers or clothing.

So get ready to attack stains when they happen with Ready Stain Remover. Stains may be here forever, but so is Ready Stain Remover: your first defense in fighting stains. Ready Stain Remover...R. C. Wilson, a family company

Now here is the script marked up:

Home Product: Ready Stain Remover

Announcer:

Stains. / They're / a part of life. / Food stains / on your / favorite shirt. Grass stains / from wrestling / with the kids. / Grease stains / from / changing the oil / in your car. / Stains / may be / here to stay / but now / you can / clean them away / with / Ready / Stain Remover.

Ready / Stain Remover /contains / special / scientifically / engineered / enzymes / that / react / with / your stain / to / break it up / and / remove it / with / a simple / wash. / Just apply / when / you spill, / rub, /or grind something / onto / your clothes. / Ready / goes to work / in seconds.

The stain / starts to fade / and / after washing, / disappears / altogether. / And Ready / is not allergenic, / so it's safe / to put / even / on baby's / diapers / or clothing.

So / get ready / to attack / stains / when / they happen / with Ready / Stain Remover. / Stains / may be here / forever / but / so is / Ready / Stain Remover: / your / first defense / in fighting / stains. / Ready / Stain Remover / …R. C. / Wilson, / a family / company.

Feeling hungry?

Restaurant Spot: Deep City Chicken – Unmarked

To get really delicious fried chicken, you gotta go deep…to Deep City Chicken. Our special herbs and spices will get you in deep—deep with flavor and deep with moist juicy chicken better than Momma used to make. Try our double deep secret recipe: Cajun-style chicken that will pepper your taste buds with flavors that will have you crying for more. You know you want it, so get in deep, with Deep City Chicken.

With food spots, you are looking for romance words—descriptive adjectives that explain your product. Try marking this one up and then check out my markings. If you have other ideas on how to mark the script, go for it. Just make sure you have the phrases broken down so they are easier to read.

Restaurant Spot: Deep City Chicken – Marked Up

To get / really / delicious / fried chicken, / you gotta / go deep / …to / Deep City / Chicken. / Our / special / herbs / and spices / will get you / in deep— / deep / with flavor / and deep / with / moist / juicy / chicken / better than / Momma used to make. / Try our / double / deep secret / recipe: / Cajun-style / chicken / that will / pepper / your taste buds / with flavors / that will have you / crying for more. / You know / you want it, / so / get in deep, / with / Deep City / Chicken.

ULTIMATE VOICEOVER TIP!

Move into the microphone for romance words.

When doing certain spots, you will notice what are called *romance words*. These are words that aptly describe the benefits or the excitement of using a specific product. It could be a word like *juicy* or simply *delicious*. It might be a word like *luxurious* for a hotel or spa. When you see such words in your script, move in just a bit on the mike and lower your voice a bit to accent the word and make it more intimate.

Dialogue: Family Scene – Unmarked

Woman: I am a wife and mother of three. They all make a mess. A big mess—every day—and I have to clean it.

Man: Who are you talking to, honey? Wait a minute. Are you on TV or something? Is this one of those reality TV shows? (excited) Kids. Get in here. We are on TV.

Girl: We are on TV? Cool. Oh, wait till I tell Marcie. She will freak!

Woman: Wait a minute.

Man: What should we do now? Act like we don't get along? Oh, let the kids jump up and down on the couch. Kids? Jump up and down and break a few things.

Boy: We can break things?

Man: Sure, it's all in the budget. Right, hon?

Woman: Budget. There's no budget.

Man: No budget? What kind of reality show is this? Get my agent on the phone.

(kids in back breaking things and making a ruckus)

Woman: Agent? You have an agent?

Man: Honey. C'mon. This is show business. We gotta have an agent. We should do a spin-off about the dog. You know how he tears things up and stuff. (laughing) Oh man. Honey, you are the best. This kicks…

Woman: Ted! There is no show.

Man: We got cancelled? Are you kidding me? Already? (yelling) Kids…I think we got cancelled.

Girl: Cancelled. Daaad. Moooom. What am I going to tell Marcie?

Woman: (exasperated) Tell her you are very sloppy and your mother has had it with all of you.

(silence)

Man: (excited) Now there is a show angle. We are...*The Sloppies*. Man, we will get a complete makeover for sure.

Boy: Can I get a jungle vine in my room?

Man: Sure. Those guys can do anything.

Ann: Communication is everything in a family. Make sure you talk to your spouse and kids every day. They need to know how you feel about things...even jungle vines in Junior's room.

Man: I'm gonna put a shooting range in the guest room for sure.

Dialogue: Family Scene – Marked Up

Woman: I am a wife / and mother / of three. / They all / make a mess. / A big mess— / every day— / and I have / to clean it.

Man: Who /are you / talking to, / honey? / Wait a minute. / Are you / on TV / or something? / Is this / one of those / reality / TV shows? / (excited) Kids. / Get in here. / We are on TV.

Girl: We are on / TV? / Cool. / Oh, wait till I / tell Marcie. / She will / freak!

Woman: Wait a minute.

Man: What should we / do now? / Act like / we don't / get along? / Oh, / let the kids / jump / up and down / on the couch. / Kids? / Jump / up and down / and break / a few things.

Boy: We can / break things?

Man: Sure, / it's all / in the budget. / Right, / hon?

Woman: Budget. / There's / no budget.

Man: No budget? / What kind of / reality show / is this? / Get / my agent / on the phone.

(kids in back breaking things and making a ruckus)

Woman: Agent? / You have / an <u>agent</u>? /

Man: Honey /. C'mon. / This is / show business. / We gotta / have an agent. / We should do / a spin-off / about / the dog. / You know / how he / tears things up / and stuff. / (laughing) Oh man. Honey, / you are the best. This / kicks / a / (cut off)

Woman: Ted! / There is / no show.

Man: We got / cancelled? / Are you / kidding me? / Already? / (yelling) Kids / …I think / we got / cancelled.

Girl: Cancelled? / Daaad. / Moooom. / What / am I / going to tell / <u>Marcie?</u>

Woman: (exasperated) Tell her / you are / very sloppy / and / your mother / has had it / with / all of you.

(silence)

Man: (excited) Now there / is a / show angle. / We are / ...*The Sloppies.* / Man, / we will / get a / complete makeover / for sure.

Boy: Can I / get a / jungle vine / in my room?

Man: Sure. / Those guys / can do / anything.

Man: I'm / gonna / put a / shooting range / in / the guest room / for sure.

Self-Improvement: Education Spot – Unmarked

Everyone wants to make more money. But you work full-time. So how is that going to happen? Finances 101 at Travis University is the answer to all your questions and needs. Finances 101 creates a curriculum that is available online or at several locations around the city. So you can create a program that works for you, when and where you want to take it.

Self-Improvement: Education Spot – Marked Up

Everyone / wants / to make more money. But you / work / full-time? So how / is that / going to happen? / Finances 101 / at Travis University / is the answer / to all your questions / and needs. / Finances 101 / creates a curriculum / that is available / online / or / at several locations / around the city. / So / you can create / a program / that works for you, / when / and where / you want to take it. / It's that easy.

Now *You* Mark It Up

Finances 101 handles everything from creating a working budget for you and your family to getting started in a home business. Classes also include the basics of being a twenty-first-century entrepreneur, planning for an early retirement, and handling finances after an illness or death in the family. It does it all, and it's there for you twenty-four hours a day and seven days a week.

See How It Matches

Finances 101 / handles everything / from creating / a working budget / for you / and your family / to getting you started / in a home business. / Classes / also include / the basics / of being / a twenty-first-century / entrepreneur, / planning / for an early retirement / and / handling finances / after an illness / or / death in the family. / It does it all, / and it's / there for you / twenty-four hours a day and / seven days a week.

Mark This One, Too

Call and one of our helpful operators will direct you to a program that works best for your specific needs. Don't wait. Call 847-902-8888 today and get started on a brighter future. Everyone wants to make more money, and with Finances 101 at Travis University, it's money made and money well spent. Finances 101. Call 847-902-8888 now and let your new life begin.

Call / and one of our / helpful operators / will direct you / to a program / that works best / for your / specific needs. / Don't wait. / Call / 847-902-8888 / today / and get started / on a / brighter future. / Everyone / wants to make / more money, / and with Finances 101 / at Travis University / it's money made / and money well spent. / Finances 101. Call 847-902-8888 now and let your new life begin.

Good job! Now you know the ins and outs of properly marking your script. This is one of the vital steps in getting in control of the script.

ULTIMATE VOICEOVER TIP!

Mark up your copy but flow through it when you read.

Even though we are giving the read piece by piece, it still needs to flow through as a single thought about buying this product. Inhale and exhale the copy if you are finding the read choppy because of the markings.

Sloppy Copy Read Alert!!!

Problem: Not reading copy points cleanly.
Solution: Read copy points backward in a sentence.

I believe in working with the brain as it functions, not how I wish it would function. I don't fight how it works. For example, the brain reads from left to right. Sometimes it skips over copy too fast in this movement. I also know that the brain does not read right to left unless your are reading Hebrew. So if I mark up copy and give the copy points backward, it will land cleanly and definitively on each copy point without blending toward the next copy point.

First USA Finer Things Platinum Visa Card

Marked:

First USA / Finer Things / Platinum / Visa Card

Read backward:

Visa Card Platinum Finer Things First USA

Now forward again:

First USA Finer Things Platinum Visa Card

The brain likes to imitate. So if you have clean copy points, when you straighten it out, you will get a clean read. Try this next one:

Bankrate.com national average bank loan rate.

Marked:

Bankrate.com / national average / bank loan / rate

Read backward:

Bank loan rate / national average / Bankrate.com

Now forward again:

Bankrate.com / national average / bank / loan / rate.

E. Practice Repeat Words

Introducing saver fares from AirTran Airways.
With saver fares you get the price you want now.
Saver fares from AirTran take you anywhere you want to go.
Saver fares from AirTran. The cheapest, best way to fly!

When you approach this copy, underline *saver fares* wherever it occurs. Change your inflection on each instances for variety. You can pick up up inflection, middle or even inflection, down inflection, and a slow or fast approach.

Read one with an up inflection and the next with a down inflection. Slow down for the one after that, and do the last one even.

Let your eye move down the page, bouncing from similar phrase to similar phrase. This will get you comfortable with reading the copy.

The Geography of a Script

A script is constructed in a certain way. It is important to see what you have ahead of you before you dig into the read. Watch for repeat words, hard-to-pronounce words, and similar-looking words like *customer* and *consumer* that might be read alike. Practice these elements first before doing a whole read. It will speed up your understanding of the copy.

Try this one out. Underline the *someone* wherever it occurs and do different inflections for each. You want to do this before you attempt to read all of the copy. It lays the foundation for a great read.

Up

Someone who doesn't sell you more if the right coverage for you costs less.

Down

Someone who understands you want quick and easy but more importantly you want it right.

Even

Someone who knows that good coverage is more than just getting that card you toss in your glove box. More than just a fifteen-minute click through to check it off your list.

Slow

Someone who's inventive, forward thinking, and always anticipating your needs.

Fast

Someone who understands the dynamics of a good investment you stay with a long time.

A different inflection is needed for each *someone* in this script to prevent monotony.

F. Cold Read

Cruise through the script to see if your markings are clear and ultimately helpful. Start at the top line with the slow hello—do it nice and easy. Then pick up pace and finish strong. Your timing can be a little slower here at first. You will pick up time as you go.

- **Do a cold read (slowly).** Get your confidence up by just getting through the script once. Make sure your script markings are not messy or confusing.

ULTIMATE VOICEOVER TIP!
The first read is always for you.

Ask any engineer. Seldom if ever is the first read ever used in the final spot. Why? The engineer is getting proper voice levels, and the creative may not be fully listening yet or perhaps still eating lunch. Knowing this, you get a freebie—a mulligan to just get comfortable. So take it by doing a leisurely read, a few seconds slower perhaps. Don't worry. You will make up the time easily. After this, do the following:

- **Do a regular timed read (close to the time needed for the spot).** Move through the script a bit faster to get closer to time.

- **Establish the correct script speed (compress your breath for a faster read).**

- **Record full reads of copy**. Now you should be able to glide through the copy; if you make a mistake, take a two-beat and then pick up the line again and continue. Do not stop. Finish the take to establish continuity.

ULTIMATE VOICEOVER TIP!

During an audition or session, don't overthink it; put your brain in a box.

No thinking is allowed—or speaking out loud, for that matter. During a voiceover session or audition, the object is to let yourself be led to the correct read for the spot in front of you. This direction will put you in the running for booking the commercial. That said, you need to leave your critical or analyzing brain outside before you enter the recording booth. Overthinking things can be a real detriment to the process of recording a commercial spot.

First off, you were hired as a voiceover talent, not a writer or a commercial critic. Your job is to simply do what the specs of the spot say and be directed—move like a hand puppet to the place the writer wants you to be. Back in the day, many homes in my neighborhood had old rabbit-ear TV antennae covered with tinfoil. Your dad would have you move those antenna ears back and forth until you got the perfect reception. You didn't offer any resistance. You just did what you were told.

The same goes in the studio setting. Let the writer or director move you in your read from side to side until he or she gets the perfect read.

Keep that critical or analyzing mind in a box outside the recording-booth door, and while you're at it, put self-criticism and apologies for mistakes out there, too.

Just keep reading with the direction of the session's director. Let the director lead you to where he or she needs you to go, and all will be well.

G. Revise

Clean up any markings that distracted you. Read again. Make sure you can now get through the copy with ease. If you stumble, slow down.

ULTIMATE VOICEOVER TIP!

When you make a mistake, it means you should slow down.

This is simple and easy. Just know that when you make a mistake, it is because you were going through your copy points too fast. Go back and grab the info more slowly, and then you can speed up. No, it is not because you suck and are unfit for this business. If you were running after a moving train, it would have to slow down to pick you up, and then and only then could it move quickly with you on it or, in this case, on the spot. Which reminds me…

ULTIMATE VOICEOVER TIP!

If you want to go fast, go slow.

If you want to be done quickly, read slowly and grasp the information. You will produce a better spot faster this way. There is a tendency to want to read a mile a minute out of the gate to impress or to get your work done faster. Relax. Do the slow cold read and build up speed naturally. As I said before, we learn everything in life slow to fast, so we are not going to buck the trend here. My goal is to get you totally relaxed and grounded in your work.

When you stare at your copy stand with your copy for a while, your read may start to lose its freshness as you take the variety of directions from the creatives. Your first read often comes out like butter because you are free and easy. So how do we return to that feeling? Glad you asked.

ULTIMATE VOICEOVER TIP!

Turn away from the page before reading again for a fresher read.

Looking at the copy can get a bit myopic or cause tunnel vision. So, to imitate the first free and easy read, turn away from the copy, count to three, and then read your next take. Reboot your brain here. You will find you get a different, fresher sound and provide more variety for your audition selection takes and your session takes.

ULTIMATE VOICEOVER TIP!

Take your headset off for real conversational reads.

If you have a real conversational read like the one above, take off your headset completely or keep them off your ears a bit to let yourself get lost in the spot and not be so "on" with your read. Being "on" means really putting in a lot of needless energy that makes what you are saying sound fake.

ULTIMATE VOICEOVER TIP!

Read the last line first and then begin the spot to establish the right tone.

It isn't easy to begin a spot out of silence. Your slate and trigger words can get you started. Sometimes reading the last line of the commercial can give you the right energy. Just do the last line, take a beat, and then do the rest. You will find a nice flow this way.

H. Write the Point of the Script in One Simple Sentence

Your script has a lot of words but one simple message. It may be "Sears is having a great sale" or "get a better night's sleep with Serta." It might be "State Farm can help you," which is as simple as you can get. If you establish this, than you will be speaking from a real point of view. When you call someone on the phone or contact someone on Facebook, you have a point—a message to give—no matter how innocuous it may be. "Just wanted to see if you got home all right" is a clean message. If you can talk from a simple POV when you start your read, everything will move nicely behind it.

Step Two of Script Reading: Read Speed

1. Begin the first line slowly to introduce the listener to the story. This is the slow hello.
2. Increase speed as you go, as if you were skiing down a hill.
3. Decelerate as you hit the last line of the script.
4. Match the speed of the top line on the last line for a book-ended approach.

1. The Slow Hello

When we first meet someone we don't know, we do what I call the *slow hello*. Use basic, slow language—simple information—not too much too soon.

For commercial reads, enter in the same way—slowly and easily—to explain what the commercial will be about.

2. Increase Speed

Like when moving down a ski hill, we pick up speed as we go. It's fastest right around the call to action, the big close: "Call today." "This offer won't last forever."

"To get your free book." "For reservations, call…"

3. Decelerate Near End

Just before the end line, begin to decelerate to give listeners a verbal cue that the spot is coming to an end. This is a common device used by great public speakers. Often they say things like "OK, so what does this tell us?" and "So to summarize what we said today…" to indicate that they are concluding their speech. These allow speakers to catch their breath and audiences to know the speaker will not be hitting them over the hit with too much information. It paces it out nicely.

You can identify these deceleration lines in commercials. It's usually something like "So the next time mosquitoes threaten your party…" or "So get the car all America is talking about…"

Look for that deceleration line, and you will be ready to finish the spot off strong.

4. Match the Last Line with the Top Line's Energy

Going back to the spot above…

> **Top Line:**
>
> Wouldn't you love to relax in a tropical desert island?
>
> **Bottom line:**
>
> Saver fares from AirTran: the only way to fly.

Just match the energy that was used at the top—relaxed and easy—at the bottom. This is a good way to practice part of the script to understand it better.

Speed Trap!

Problem: I am reading great, but I am reading too slowly.
Solution: Voice compression comes to the rescue.

I think this is a great place to mention techniques to handle the speed of our script.

The Art of Voice Compression:
How to Read Copy Fast

Commercial copy is often overwritten, requiring you to get through the copy very quickly. This is particularly true of tags—add-on copy at the end of a commercial that carries a lot of sticky legal info, including prices and percentages, which are more difficult to get through quickly. So instead of taking a big breath and hoping you don't crash and burn at the end of the page, here is a surefire way to read quickly and not pass out from oxygen deprivation: the point of this is to maximize your breath use to get through copy quicker. Like a trumpeter blowing into his mouthpiece, compressed energy allows for more words more quickly.

1. Read copy slowly and deliberately at first. Try this tongue twister: "Rubber baby buggy bumper." Say it slowly at first and then speed up until you are going quickly.

2. Compress your breath. Put your tongue behind your teeth. Make a "da da da da" sound. Take a breath and exhale your copy, shooting your words through a virtually closed mouth. This eliminates the big inhale and exhale that costs you time. Don't worry about volume. Conversational level is always best. Start there and adjust up or down slightly. Let your words rattle out by compressing your breath, squeezing it out so you can fly over the words quicker and easier.

3. Find phrases in the copy you can cluster together and read quickly. I'm going to give you a tag to practice on, but a few words before you start. The line breaks in this marked-up tag are to help you locate key phrases and focus on reading them one by one. Here it is:

Financing example
Forty-eight months
$19.05 (read as *nineteen oh five*) per month
Per thousand dollars
Financed.

Now flow them all together: "Financing example, forty-eight months, $19.05 per month, per thousand dollars financed."

Return back to the entire script. Establish a pace that you began with this sentence and go through the entire script:

Financing example, / forty-eight months, / $19.05 / per month, / per $1,000 / financed. / 25.9 percent / down payment. / Savings compare / 0.9%APR / to a banktown.com / national average / bank loan rate. Residency / restrictions / apply. You / must take / retail delivery / from participating / dealer stock / by July 18, 2015. Dealer financial participation may affect consumer cost. Not available with customer cash offers.

Remember, start slow and pick up pace. Take more time on words that don't flow easily, like *financing.*

Step Three: Script Interpretation

a. **Voice triggers.** Make a sound that triggers the tone of the spot.

b. **Start slow.** Give a basic hello, introducing the story of the product or service.
c. **Pick up your pace** as you head into the meat of the copy, the jelly in the donut.
d. **Go up on the mike.** Drop your voice for the product-feature section.
e. **Back off the mike.** Use a regular volume to conclude the spot.
f. **Alter line speeds.** Use different speeds line to line and within lines themselves for variety or a manual read. Do two lines and then change.
g. **Find script nuances.** Find how things are said differently (e.g., internal monologues versus straight deliveries, elements of sarcasm or teasing, etc.)

A. Voice Triggers

Here's a thought: Everything you need is in your voice—every emotion and every attitude. You just need to rediscover this in front of the microphone. There are ways to unleash this natural ability.

ULTIMATE VOICEOVER TIP!

Wave your arms, raise your eyebrows, and point your fingers. Let your body do the talking.

Your body can trigger a lot of what you need emotionally in your reads. So be alive in front of the microphone. Just don't hit anything!

Voice triggers and ramp-ups come to the rescue. Has anyone ever told you that you sound tired, happy, or sad? Of course, you didn't get on the phone to sound that way; it was just naturally in your voice. You didn't need to take an acting class to express it either. It was just there. You don't go around talking with a big announcer-type voice unless you are some kind of freakazoid. That said, how do you access these emotions in a timely fashion to create a killer audition? The answer is voice triggers.

Voice triggers allow us to tap into that natural energy without acting up a storm. A voice trigger is a short expression said before you read a spot that matches the style required in your copy.

For instance, for a sarcastic read, you could say, "Yeah, right," perhaps rolling your eyes for effect. Let's say the first line of your copy is "Did you remember your wife's anniversary this year?" It needs to be delivered in a sarcastic tone. So you would say, "Yeah, right," take a beat, and then say, "Did you remember your wife's anniversary this year?" What this does is it catches your voice in a flow so you are not so conscious of what you are saying. This is achieved many times when we read copy three times in a row. We lose ourselves in the copy and speak normally, not paying attention to each thing we say.

For an upbeat, energetic read, you could say, "Wow!" When you do this, your eyes open wider, your energy rises, and you don't have to fake being excited. Many times our energy is below what is necessary for a spot. These triggers quickly get us where we need to be.

Let's say the first line of your copy is "It's the all-new Shamu show at Sea World. Where you learn to really believe!"

Just say, "Wow," take a beat, and then deliver the line. You will find you will be there automatically without a lot of direction and needless takes. Again, as I mentioned, you know how to be excited. These triggers get you there immediately.

For a caring and concerned read—like, for example, a children's hospital spot—you could quietly say, "Oh...I hope she's OK." This puts you in a quieter, more caring place with your voice. Let's say a line in the hospital spot is "You want what's best for your children. And that means having the best pediatric care. Like the caring hands of Amster Children's hospital."

By saying "Oh, I hope he's OK," you are showing empathy already upon starting the spot. This prevents a clichéd read or one that makes fun of the spot.

You should notice I've said *could* instead of *would* to guide you to a choice that I have seen work as a trigger in many recordings. However, if you have your own ideas, have at it. Just say your trigger word, give a beat or pause, and then deliver the copy as written. You need that pause in there so it doesn't present an editing problem for your engineer. You don't want him glaring at you as he tries to cut out your trigger word too close to the actual copy.

Other triggers include the following:

> **Voice of God**: **"Helllllloooo down there!"** perhaps while cupping your hands around your mouth.
>
> **Cool, younger voice: "Heyyyy, dude" or "Ohhhh yeahhhhh."** Do these quietly and up on the microphone.
>
> **Sophisticated voice**: **"Yes, yes, marvelous, delightful, delicious."**
>
> **Sexy female voice**: **"Heyyyy, sexy."** Do this up on the microphone and quiet.
>
> **Big attitude: "Hey, dumbass."** This may sound crude, but it will make you laugh and relax, which will make the read get better. Try it!

Experiment: Voice Trigger as a Nerves Killer

Read one take without the trigger initially and then add it for the second one and see how it changes your read. We need to catch you in motion—that is why the trigger works so well. It allows you to platform into the read. Also you will not be so conscious of getting started or hearing your first words in front of the mike, and you will not feel much nervousness or anticipation.

Voice Triggers for Speed: To Slow Down

This is pretty basic stuff. Just do a slow countdown to slow you down—"3…2…1…"—and then read your copy. Remember to keep the numbers spread out. Some of my students blow through the countdown too fast, defeating the purpose of it altogether. Keep it measured and wait for a beat before each count. Then talk. Remember to keep a space before the actual copy to be recorded to prevent editing problems.

Ramp-Ups: For Cleaner, More Genuine Reads

Reading a script from a silent start can be difficult. We expect ourselves to land perfectly on the first line and create magic on down the script. This could happen, but why not make it easier (or, dare I say, stupidly easy?) with a ramp-up line or lines. Consider the following script:

Sky Winds Restaurant

Fine dining has never been like this. See the city as you never have before: in elegance at Sky Winds Restaurant on the ninety-eighth floor of the Merrill Tower. Romantic, breathtaking, and the finest haute cuisine that the city has to offer.

We could just plunge in after the engineer says "take one" into our headphones. But we could try a different method: ramping up into the spot. Just say a line or lines to yourself before the take begins. It can be something like "Wow, I have to tell you about this restaurant. It is amazing!" Wait a beat or two and then begin the spot. Make sure the ramp-up has the same energy. What this does is it catches you in motion, which is easier than talking from a dead start. Try it with the above spot, and then see how it works with this one:

> **Amicable Insurance**
>
> A family means so many things: love, respect, fun, and a whole lot of financial responsibility. It's easy to get overwhelmed with the day-to-day and long-term needs of your family like health insurance and money for college. Let us help. We're Amicable, and we know how it feels.

A possible ramp-up for this would be the following: "Boy, I'm glad I used Amicable Insurance. They really helped us out."

What the ramp-up does is get you into the mood or note of the script so you have already arrived once the real copy starts. I find it easier to do most things while in motion, so why not apply this to reading commercial copy?

So where do you do this ramp-up business? Do it just to the side of the mike, sort of as an aside before you begin a new take. It might go like this:

> You: "Boy, I'm glad I used Amicable Insurance. They really helped us out."
> Engineer: "OK, let's do another one. Take three!"
> You: "A family means so many things…"

That's it: simple and easy to do. Just make sure your ramp-up matches the energy of the spot. Don't do a "wow" beginning for a quieter spot, like for a hospital or luxury car. Take your time. Never rush. Just lay it out there, smooth and easy.

B. Start Slow

ULTIMATE VOICEOVER TIP!

Always read the first line of your copy more slowly than the rest.

As we mentioned in Part II, this allows you to ease into the copy you are reading. The first line of a commercial is a type of greeting or intro to tell audiences about the story you are about to tell. By laying out line one in an easy, relaxed manner, the listener can grab hold of what you are saying and follow the rest of the copy more easily. Remember, if you are having trouble slowing down, perform a countdown.

The first line of the script is the pace line of the copy. Read that line at a leisurely pace, get grounded in the spot, and move quicker as you go. We learn everything in life from slow to fast, and there's no need to reinvent the wheel. If you start too fast, it will only get faster. If you nab the right speed, you will be locked in and then control the script the rest of the way.

C. Pick Up Pace

Just like a skier, when you start moving downhill, the speed increases. This is no different from when you speak with someone. You get more animated, talk faster, and give more descriptive or intimate details as you progress in the conversation.

With your script, after the initial slow hello, we start to move into the guts of the spot—the jelly in the donut, so to speak.

ULTIMATE VOICEOVER TIP:

You will naturally gain speed as you go.

From the time we learn to walk as children, we learn everything slow to fast. So why make this process any different? It is natural for us to do this and unnatural to attack the script in one big gulp. It is sort of like running out onto a skating rink after not having skated in a while. It takes a few laps to get the blood flowing and the muscle memory back. So always read your first take slowly to get comfortable with the script. With familiarity you will gain speed. That is a given. With each take, you will gain speed as you gain familiarity with the script. This happens naturally so you don't have to goose the script or hit it too hard.

Here are some survival tips. Trust this process:

1. Break down the copy to smaller points.
2. Start reading slowly and then moving faster with familiarity.
3. If making mistakes, focus and slowly read missed copy points.
4. Regain speed.
5. Step away from the mike on occasion to refresh your brain.
6. Drink apple juice, eat apple pieces, or sip water to keep mouth noise away.
7. If you feel jangled or nervous, slow your read down until comfortable.
8. If it is really grinding, hit the restroom. Splash water in your face and return.

D. Up on the Mike

As you get into the sell of the spot—the place with all the descriptions of how the product works or will make your life better in some way—you should move toward the mike and lower your volume. This is especially true when you see the words *you* and *your*.

All commercials are a series of statements and intimate statements. You are telling the audience—the potential buyer—various statements about the product. Consider the following example:

> Everyone wants to make more money. With the cost of living going up, it's important to find new forms of income. But you work full-time and have a family—how are you going to make more money?
>
> At the Marcus School of Business, you can learn how to make more money even with your current busy lifestyle. It all starts with a call. Call today, and one of our trained assistants will work out a plan that will have you getting more out of life.

OK. Here are the statements:

Everyone wants to make more money. With the cost of living going up, it's important to find new forms of income. It all starts with a call.

These are general statements, thoughts, and pieces of information for all to hear. They initially approach the entire audience to send a comprehensive net out to all who are listening. Then we start getting personal.

Here are the intimate statements:

But you work full-time and have a family—how are you going to make more money? At the Marcus School of Business, you can learn how to make more money even with your current busy lifestyle. Call today and one of our trained assistants will work out a plan that will have you getting more out of life.

So what is the difference between each of these statement styles?

It is the words *you* and *your.* When you see these words, just lean in on the mike a bit to change the sound of the spot. The sound will become more personal, more intimate, and more directed at the individual. You will find this in many spots. This technique is a stupidly easy way to nuance your copy and provide variety to your read.

When you get to the body of the copy—the part where the product or service is described—you should lean in and lower your voice a bit to provide contrast. Most times these will be television spots so you will be watching the visual and won't need a pushed voice telling you what you can see with your own two eyes.

On my UltimateVoiceover.com website, there is a free lesson that addresses this issue. Check it out! Did I say it was free?

Let's take a look at this spot:

Ready Stain Remover

(regular fuller voice read)
Stains. They're a part of life. Food stains on your favorite shirt. Grass stains from wrestling with the kids. Grease stains from changing the oil in your car. Stains may be here to stay, but now you can clean them away with Ready Stain Remover.

(product sell lean in; quieter)
Ready Stain Remover contains special scientifically engineered enzymes that react with your stain to break it up and remove it with a simple wash. Just apply when you spill, rub or grind something onto your clothes. Ready goes to work in seconds.

(regular fuller voice read)
So get ready to attack stains when they happen with Ready Stain Remover. Stains may be here forever, but so is Ready Stain Remover: your first defense in fighting stains. Ready Stain Remover...R. C. Wilson, a family company.

It reminds me of my old science teacher who would first address the class in a full voice and then shut off the lights and speak over the action on the screen much more quietly. Then she would say, "Turn on the lights please," and finish with the class in full voice again.

E. Back off the Mike

Make a *C* shape with your forefinger and thumb. That is how far away from the microphone you should be when you start your read. Opening lines that contain statements—not intimate statements with *you* or *your* in them—are read away from the mike. You lean in for the body copy and product descriptions, as shown above.

Then return to your original to end your spot as well, finishing strong that *C* distance from the mike. Get used to this subtle in-and-out movement. Practice it as soon as you get in front of the microphone.

F. Alter Line Speeds

Remember, you are a storyteller. To keep your audience's interest, you have to vary your read. One way to do this is with line-speed changes. By altering your line speeds, you engage yourself and the listener in a more interesting way.

Lately, in my teaching, I have discovered the concepts of manual and automatic reads. A manual read is much preferred for commercial copy. Here is what I mean.

It seems to me that our brains love to go on automatic, doing chores over and over again without much thought. Imagine your car ride back from work where you don't even remember the ride even though you took countless turns to get home. Now imagine the first time you took that ride. You watched every street sign or exit off the highway. You drove slowly to make sure you did not overshoot your location. This is true for the first time we travel anywhere. We are on manual, looking around and being aware at all times or else risking getting lost. Also think about how engaged you are driving a stick shift (manual) versus automatic.

When it comes to reading a script, it is vitally important that we connect with the listener—the person listening on the radio or television. The way to do this is to vary your read using the following reading styles:

- Speed: fast, slow, even.
- Inflection: high, low, even.
- Movement: in on mike, back off mike.
- Voice volume: up, down.
- Line splits: different speeds for each section of line.

By applying these script-reading styles, you go on manual mode so that the script is not rote. You keep the mind engaged by shifting speeds and inflections and by moving in on and off the mike. You never want to memorize your script. This leaves you less open to direction because you will have passed over into automatic mode.

Let's takes these voice reading styles out for a ride. First, take a look at this sample script:

TRICOM Cable

It's the TRICOM triple play: three great services for the price of one.

All new customers can get great Internet, cable, and phone service for a single monthly bill of just $79.99. That's right. $79.99!

Why pay more for individual services when we can bundle them for you in one exciting offer? The TRICOM triple play: Internet, cable, and phone together for $79.99.

All you have to do is call 1-800-WANT-TRICOM and an installer will be at your house to get you set up. The TRICOM triple play.

You've never had it so good!

Now practice it with the voice reading styles indicated.

TRICOM Cable

(inflect up) (read faster) (read slower)
It's the TRICOM triple play: / three great services / for the price of one.

(read slow, inflect down) (read faster)
All new customers / can get great Internet, cable, and phone

(read slower) (read faster)
service / for a single monthly bill of just $79.99. / That's right. $79.99!

(in on mike) (read slower)
Why pay more for individual services / when we can bundle them for you in

(read slower) (read faster and inflect up at end)
one exciting offer? / The TRICOM triple play: Internet, cable, and phone together for $79.99.

(in on the mike)
All you have to do is call 1-800- WANT-TRICOM / and an installer will be your house to get you set up

(read slower, inflect even) (inflect down)
The TRICOM triple play. You've never had it so good.

This example should give you a sense of how you can vary speeds and inflections as well as your position on the microphone during recording. This markup does not indicate the only way of doing things—this is just an example to show you how you can vary the read and make it more manual than automatic.

Now try out these voice reading styles on a piece of narration copy:

> The year was 1932. The United States was plunged into a crippling depression. After the stock market crash of 1929, banks were closing, business shuttered their doors, and millions of American wandered in search of work. For newly elected president of the United States Franklin Delano Roosevelt, this was a challenge, one to match or perhaps exceed his recovery from crippling polio earlier in his life. How could he get the country's economy to rebound?
>
> (fast, inflect up) (slower, even inflect)
> The year was 1932.
>
> (faster) (slower, end with inflect down)
> The United States was plunged / into a crippling depression.
>
> (fast, inflect down) (slower, inflect down)
> After the stock market crash of 1929, / banks were closing,
>
> (fast) (slow, even) (slow, down)
> businesses shuttered their doors, / and millions of Americans wandered /
>
> (fast, down) (fast, even) (slow, even)
> in search of work. For newly elected / president of the United States
>
> (fast, down) (slow, even) (fast, even)
> Franklin Delano Roosevelt, this was a challenge, one to match /

(fast, even) (slow, even) (faster, down)
or perhaps exceed / his recovery / from crippling polio / earlier in his life.

(fast, even) (fast, up)
How could he get / the country's economy / to rebound?

Now you try using this formatting on your readings. You don't have to put all these markings on the scripts. Just make sure you know you have the options given and learn to mix them into your reading so you have a present manual read instead of one where you check out and go on automatic. Good luck.

By altering your line speeds, you will become a more interesting storyteller, one who keeps his or her audience attentive by not settling into a predictable pace. This process also keeps you engaged in the copy and not just reading lines one after another. For a more interesting commercial, line-speed changes get the job done.

G. Find Script Nuances

A nuance is a subtle difference or distinction in expression, meaning, or response.

As you get a good, solid, consistent read, you want to be able to spin the words a bit here and there to give some different texture to the read. Ever see a great pool player or bowler finesse his or her shot with a body movement to add some flair to his or her game? That is what I want from you: some finesse or nuance in your read.

What I need you to do is find in the script—usually more toward the bottom—a phrase or word you can spin in a different way that breaks out from the copy. We don't want everything to be the same and sound monotonous. It should spring out and keep us alert. Consider this:

> Marco's gives you, the sports fan, what you truly want: an all-inclusive spot to hang with friends, have a few beers, and enjoy all your favorite sports action.
>
> Our food isn't half-bad either.

The first part of this spot is very informational. It tells us where to go to get great sports action. It lists what games are on and so forth.

This section gets more personal. The first part of many spots gives general information and the name of the sports bar. This section makes it personal and more intimate. It relates to you individually, not just part of the group. Notice the word *you* in this section. This is a simple key to changing your read.

I call it "leaning into your read." On my website UltimateVoiceover.com, there is a free lesson on leaning into your copy. It usually occurs on the words *you* and *your* in a script, and it is done very simply: just move in on the microphone a bit and lower your voice to compensate for being closer to it. It is like talking directly into the listener's ear. It makes it very direct, very intimate, and very personal. This is a script nuance.

A script nuance can be a speeding up or slowing down of copy—a contrast to the rest of the commercial.

> So you sit there like the smallest kid in gym class and watch them ask for big shoes and longer jeans, and it hits you.

This line, taken from an insurance spot, allows the reader to have some fun with the interpretation. I see this as a type of stand-up read, glib compared to all the product information and solutions to come. Just move through it quickly and throw it off as it rattles out of your mouth.

The fast lane...just got a speed limit.

A quick, punchy one-liner that breaks out at the end of a thirty-second commercial.

What are you waiting for? Get in the car and drive to paradise today.

A traveling spot allows you to have some fun telling the listener to make the decision to go to warm, sunny Florida.

The script nuance is a little spice on the food—avoid too much because it will get too showy. Just insert a little bit of contrast to make the spot more engaging after you have done all the dirty work laying out the product features. Look for nuances after you have established everything else on your checklist. It's that little extra that will distinguish you over others. It just might get you the job.

Bleaching the Read: A Personal Anecdote

A while back I was cast for an Einstein Bagels spot to do a George W. Bush read. It had all the cadence of a good impression of President Bush, and I got the job in this comedic spot.

In the session, I read my part, and the writer picked up her head and said, "Uh, let's not do that Southern thing." Hmm. First, Bush is not Southern, and the voice I did had gotten me the part. So what did I do?

Option 1:

Read the voice without the accent.

Option 2:

Read the voice with the same accent and be obstinate.

Option 3:

Bleach the voice.

I chose Option 3. Here is why: I had auditioned for the part and won it with my approach. If I abandoned the voice altogether, then I would have gotten over directed and ended up with a voice choice that was not unique. I had gotten picked from a field of hundreds, so I wanted to hold on to what had gotten me there.

There is a very good chance I could have been replaced for the run of the spot if I had changed the voice too much. That is not good. So I gave them a bleached-out version of the voice. I kept the style in the beginning and end of the voice. In the middle, I toned it down. It worked. At the end of the spot, I added in the full taste of the voice. The spot was funny, and everyone was satisfied.

ULTIMATE VOICEOVER TIP!

Protect your audition and protect your session.

It takes a lot to win an audition. If your voice matches the voice in the mind of the writer, it is special indeed. So you don't want to abandon it because a young writer wants to change your read. If you give over to what I call "the hall of infinite possibilities," they may pull you by the nose all over the session only to replace you for the run of the spot. So you need to be conscious of how much you are lightening or bleaching out your choice—don't abandon it altogether. It was approved by the client, who may not be there. You want your spot to run so you get residuals with a union contract. You may get paid for the session but not for the run, where the big money is, so my advice is to protect your audition and protect your session.

PART IV: The Script

SUMMARY

- Mark up your scripts.
- Start with a basic "talking into cell phone" read.
- Start slow and pick up speed naturally.
- Make a mistake? Slow down.
- Vary your read speeds for a quality read.
- Use voice triggers and ramp-ups to capture tone.
- Look away before reading again to trigger fresh reads.

PART V
Getting Hired

- Where does the work come from?
- Making and maintaining contacts.
- What you can and cannot control.
- Voiceover roadblocks.
- The audition.
- The voiceover session.
- Promotion and branding.

Where Does the Work Come from?

I have always felt that a voiceover's workflow is like a stock portfolio. There is everything from basic consistent work (money market, CDs, etc.) to the most speculative, highest-paying work (mercurial stocks) and everything in between (mutual funds).

In the voiceover business, there can be jobs of all different pay scales. Some provide consistent lower-paying work. Some are high-paying infrequent jobs—usually national radio or television spots. Internet clients may provide well-paying non broadcast work. It all counts. It all pays, and we want to establish each beachhead over time.

After you have trained yourself to be in this business, you can be hired across many different platforms; the more, the better. Each stream of income helps keep you afloat in the VO business as you continue to audition and invest in yourself along the way.

I am going to name the common sources of income in the voiceover business. Keep in mind that you only get paid once you get cast and are hired for a voice session either in a professional studio or your home studio. Auditions are always free and sent in to achieve exposure and eventually get you cast. Unless you are known from previous work and they want to hire you outright, you will audition the script and then be cast if you are the right person for the job.

Audition to Voiceover Session

In this most common scenario, you are sent a script to audition and record, either at home or at your voice agent's office. You submit your audition and then are cast to play the part (e.g., announcer, man 1, woman 1, etc.) in a voiceover session.

This audition comes from your voiceover agent or from a website (e.g., Voice123, Voices.com, etc.). Upon completion, you will receive payment in the mail, in person at your agent's, or via a PayPal account you set up to receive your pay. This should occur within two to three weeks. SAG-AFTRA union contracts have a stipulated shorter timeframe, usually around two weeks. With nonunion work, there can be a delay or even a failure to pay with disreputable clients. Usually, though, this is not the case.

Direct and Repeat Bookings

In this scenario, you can be rehired again for a client on the basis of your excellent work on other commercials or projects. This requires no audition since they know your voice and professional approach from meeting and working with you in-session. This might occur if you are the voice of an ad campaign or product for the agency (e.g., the announcer for Off! bug spray, BMO Harris Bank, etc.). Another wrinkle on this is a close friend or colleague hiring you outright to do a voiceover session for them. They would know your sound from your demo and personal encounters.

Lift

In this scenario, you have done a commercial for a client, and they have lifted part of it to create a new commercial. No audition or session is required in that they are using recorded material to create a new commercial or program. For instance, you may do a tag (legal info) for a commercial for BMO Harris Bank. They take your tag and add it to three new commercials. You will get paid for three new commercials while you are taking your dog for a walk or cruising the grocery aisle. This is the best of the best.

As a member of SAG-AFTRA, you need not worry about this. It will happen, if needed, automatically, and you will be paid again for the use of your voice. In a nonunion setting, this could be written in the buyout, which means the client gets usage of your voice for other work and pays you a fee for that right. In this setting, it never hurts to ask your agent about future use. Traditionally, though, it is specified for usage of your voice.

The Money Flow: Streams of VO Income

- Broadcast
    - TV commercials
    - Radio commercials
    - Promos (promoting upcoming programs)

- Narration (for programming)

This is the most common form of VO income, the reason why most of us got into the business: traditional commercials for TV and radio and narration and promo for television. I have done all these, and each one brings a separate set of challenges and monetary rewards.

TV

Traditional union television commercials can be very lucrative if they have long runs and play a lot on network television. In this case, you would like to see them on the traditional CBS, NBC, ABC, and FOX networks for the best income. You'll make money in two ways.

Session fees are what you are paid for recording the commercial, and residual fees are what you are paid for the run of the commercial (this is union-only). Your spot can run for a period of thirteen weeks or so and then get renewed. At this point you would get paid again. If the spot is used after a three-year period, it can be renegotiated for upward of 50 to 100 percent of the original fee.

- Class A: Pay per play across the networks.
- Dealer use: All Chevy dealers pay you fees.
- Wild spot: Individual buys in various individual cities. Payment depends on units accumulated for each market. The bigger the market and the more units, the more money you will receive.
- Cable: Single payment for cable use. A multiplier of your voiceover session fee.
- Internet: So many commercials or pieces of commercials appear on the Internet now. Traditional television, especially for the millennial generation, is becoming a thing of the past. Information is accessed on phones, tablets, and laptops. Recording a commercial for the Internet will not seem much different from recording

it for broadcast television. However, the pay scale is far less. Even on a union contract, they will pay you only a fixed fee to cover use.

So you can see that in a union situation, one commercial used in all these different ways can accumulate lots of income for you.

Radio

Radio is nowhere near as lucrative but still a viable money flow. There are radio networks at which pay is better, but traditionally you get session payment and some use residuals in a union situation and a buyout—one and done—in a nonunion situation.

If you work for a radio station, you will be doing lots and lots of commercial reads for the various clients who buy time on your station. However, you will get a salary at the station that covers the myriad spots you voice and sometimes produce. You won't get paid individually for each spot like you would as a freelance voiceover announcer. Yet you can have an agent who can get you auditions and potential work outside of the station. This is the best of both worlds.

There are radio networks that may play your spot repeatedly. You will get paid for that time plus an additional fee in the future to rerun it if the mandatory three-year usage time expires and needs to be renewed.

Promos

Promos are individual announcements for upcoming programming that go like "Next up on Ellen..." Since these are time-based, there are no residuals here. Tuesday announcements are over after Tuesday ends. These are used for talk shows and TV station lineups.

Narration

Many broadcast programs need a narrator to explain the action of the show. Cable programming, especially on stations like the Discovery Channel, is filled with such programs that require voice actors to narrate the story on the screen. This usually requires a quieter, more focused sound just laying out the story points. Since there is a visual, there is no need to overamp the read. The more experienced or older voice actor usually gravitates to this area.

When you access a link while cruising the Net, you will be met with a commercial that you may one day voice.

Non-broadcast

Corporate

There is a wide variety of non-broadcast corporate voice work. It may include any of the following:

- A simple promotion of Rotary International to boost morale.
- A narration to explain the services of a company health plan.
- A quick video to explain proper cooking procedure at McDonald's.

This type of work pays a fixed hourly rate and an additional fee per half hour. At the beginning and when you enter an older age bracket, this type of work might be more attainable than high-profile network spots gobbled up by the latest celebrities and stars.

When dealing with Internet casting sites like Voice123 and Voices.com, you will find a fair amount of this type of work available. Smaller companies that need a good, solid read for a reduced price will inquire about your services. You will post your demo, and they can listen and choose you if they desire. While competitive, it is far less so than when approaching work for high-profile network spots as well as narration work. This is a great way to get started, do some work, and improve your read and ability to record and send in material.

Audiobooks

The audiobook business is currently booming with more and more titles being read by voice talent both experienced and inexperienced. There is plenty of opportunity, but the pay scale may not be to your liking. A traditional audiobook could be read by the author, an experienced audio book actor, or a regular voiceover talent. It pays a fee based on the finished amount of hours. Usually a project will be in the area of $1,500 to $2,000. However, unlike the quick hour or so of a traditional commercial, you will spend many hours recording a book as well as doing the necessary preparation of reading, mapping out voices for characters, and researching difficult terms and names. So your per-hour rate will drop the longer it takes to record.

Beginners may get work on a royalty-only basis. In this scenario, you end up with no pay for your reading and recording time but receive 25 percent per sold book.

Jeff's Advice

If you are only reading the book and are not responsible for recording, too, this is not a bad way to break in. However, if you are involved in both narrating and recording at home, then you are doing double the work for the same pay. In recording, there are a variety of tasks necessary to produce a professional recording. This takes a considerable amount of time to perform and master.

For the beginner, this may seem like a good way to get into the business and get experience, but with no direction or guidance, you may get into sloppy habits as well. There are many types of work in the voiceover business, and this is by far the most time intensive. **So think a bit before tackling a project like this, especially with a royalty format. In these cases you receive no up-front money—just a percentage of the sales. Maybe do this once or twice to get experience but not as a steady diet of work. Try not to feed the beast of low pay work for high output of time.**

Video Games

A lot of my students love gaming. They play games and think that doing voices for games would be exciting and fun. It is, but this is the most strenuous use.

Since most games are crime- and war-based, you will be screaming and dying…a lot. This puts a large strain on your vocal cords, so beware. You have to monitor and soothe your voice along the way with warm water and honey. For a main character of a typical video game, you may have two hundred lines, and recording requires three takes on each at a high-octane volume.

Pay here is by the hour or project depending on the amount of parts you play and the hours you work. A big game company like Ubisoft will pay top dollar; others may make a deal with you or your agent. Again, enjoy the work but be careful not to trash your voice.

ULTIMATE VOICEOVER TIP!

If your voice is catching or you are beginning to cough, raise up your range so you can repeat the voice in other takes without crashing.

This is crucial in general but particularly when it comes to video game work. Be diligent. You may feel fine after the job but have vocal hoarseness a day later. I saw an actor experience this, first hand. He was almost released from the job due to this malady.

Phone Prompts:

"Hello, and thanks for calling Citibank. Press one if you need customer service..."

Phone prompt work can be a nice, consistent gig in the voice business. You may do standard messages and come back to record refresher or seasonal messages. You will be paid by the hour depending on what your agent or you negotiate. Either way, it is not taxing work and can pay a few bills, being a nice, steady source of income.

In Review

These are the most common forms of voice work. As I said in the beginning, like with an investment portfolio, some (like phone prompts) pay modest consistent fees, while others (like network television commercials) can deliver great sums of money. Your job is to audition and market yourself to get in these different voiceover circles so that if one commercial is off the air, you still get income coming in. This comes over time with the many contacts you make in this business. Marketing yourself is crucial, and the more clients you connect with, the better a financial web you will weave.

To Be or Not to Be: Union versus Nonunion.

As a voiceover actor, you will be faced with the decision of being a union or nonunion talent.

First, let's look at what each of these mean and what benefits they confer.

Nonunion

- **Where do I get the work?**

  Auditions and straight bookings through non-union agents. Auditions and casting through Internet sites like Voice123 and Voices.com. Non-signatory companies.
  Personal connections.

- **Who hires you?**

  Clients are much more varied than union clients. Not SAG-AFTRA signatories. Not subject to union rules and regulations. Big and small. Internet and agency.
  Clients are not held to SAG-AFTRA contract and rules so its up to the integrity of each client to pay well and on time. No penalties for late payments.

- **Pay**

  Much more varied. Small fees to higher fees that mirror union fees. Might get paid hourly fee to execute a certain number of scripts. Might get per-script or per-program fee.

- **Residuals**

  There are no residual or repeat payments with nonunion work. You will get a lump-sum buyout that covers usage for a set period of time, usually in perpetuity. This can be a good chunk of change but lower most times than a union residual setup that renews over different periods of time.

- **Pros**

    - Can get work easier (though it is never easy).
    - Can work for a wider variety of clients. There are more sources of possible work.
    - Competitive but not as much as SAG-AFTRA work, which includes ravenous celebrity clientele.
    - Can get started through Internet sites without waiting for agent representation.
    - No dues or insurance fees.

- **Cons**

    - No repeat or residual payments for voiceover work.
    - Clients can pay late or not at all.
    - No pension or health plan offered.

Union

I admit to being biased in favor of union voice acting. I have been a member of what is now called SAG-AFTRA since 1983. The benefits have been many. Up until recently I had a medical plan with both unions (SAG and AFTRA). I also have a pension with both unions in that they were not joined when I joined back then. I feel protected by the rules and regulations of the union that keep clients on the straight and narrow. I have been paid for every job I have ever done without exception. That is amazing unto itself.

My first job as a booth announcer for children's programming was with WFLD in Chicago. When they needed to make a change to a female voice, the producer of the station tried to pull a fast one on me in terms of what benefits I was due. I told him to call the union office because I was a union announcer, which surprised him. I was offered about six weeks of pay due to two weeks' notice and vacation. This was tremendous.

And if any of my content appeared on the air, I got a week's pay. The station goofed up, and I got four more additional weeks.

Just being able to call the union gave me such comfort and a sense of protection. Since my wife was about to deliver my son Zach in a few months, it sure came in handy. I will never forget how the union helped me then and has continued to provide proper pay during my thirty-plus years in the business. SAG and AFTRA have taken good care of me and my family. And you know what? No agency budgets were in the red, and no states faced bankruptcy. No governments toppled. Everyone benefited—the actors, the advertising agencies, and the clients. We did not draw upon the public largesse but were simply paid what we were worth to everyone's financial benefit. This is a great system.

- **Pros**
    - Great pay.
    - Residual pay for airings of present and future voiceover work.
    - Working with a top-notch, reputable client base.
    - Working with the best voice actors in the business.
    - Health plan.
    - Pension plan (after vesting or reaching pay level after ten years).
    - Best working conditions and best studios and treatment.
- **Cons**
    - Membership fee due once joining the union. This costs $3,000 or more.
    - Must pay dues and health insurance fees.
    - Must be cast in a union job to join.
    - Harder to establish consistent union career.

- Celebrity encroachment for top-paying jobs.
- Unable to do non-union jobs without claiming financial core or Fi-Core.

Jeff's Advice

Start non-union and build up experience with the following:

- Auditioning
- Recording at home and sending in edited material.
- Working with clients.
- Being represented by a nonunion agent.

Register with Internet sites like Voice123 and Voices.com to get auditioning quickly and to get used to sending in recordings.

Join SAG-AFTRA union if you

- Have been cast in a union spot or series of spots that can pay or help pay the membership fee.
- Have created a client base of union signatories and want to use your talents.
- Are simply ready to move up with the big boys and girls. Have proper training and experience.

Taft-Hartley Act

If you perform a union spot, you will have to join the union on your second job. You will be "Taft-Hartleyed." The Taft-Hartley Act is a law that says you can do as many spots as you can in one month's time until you must join. If you are assured continued work, then joining the union might be for you. Otherwise, be wary not to join without adequate compensation to cover costs.

So it is vitally important not to take low-paying non-broadcast work that won't provide residual or continued pay. Otherwise you will be out the membership fee and have no hope of recouping the money. It's just not a smart choice.

Basically, that is how it works. Most of my students start nonunion and stay there or eventually segue into union work if there is a demand for their talents. If you can do union work, I say go for it. The pay is better, and you will enjoy other future benefits. However, if this is just a small side job for you, nonunion work is the way to go.

Making and Maintaining Contacts

I can't say enough about this aspect of the business. Once you have your training and demo produced, you are ready to hit the market with your talents. These talents will be in front of real-life human beings. Even though we live in a high-tech world, the human connection is the greatest thing you have going for you besides your skill set.

It is not apps or the latest gadgets on the market that hire you but people. Contacts are bigger than your agent. While he or she is vital for your success, it is the contacts you find, create, and nurture that will keep you working year after year.

ULTIMATE VOICEOVER TIP!

Start a contact list now.

Do not delay. Think of the people you may know working in the business:

- Actors.
- Friends.
- Family members.

- Agency people (writers, producers, creative directors, and art directors).
- Public relations people.
- Marketing people.
- Agents.
- Interns.
- Recording engineers.
- Casting agents.
- VO coaches and teachers.

Contact anyone who can get your demo heard. Keep them on your list. There are people out there who would love to help you. Let them. Stay in touch with them. If you are a working actor, invite them to shows to give them a night on the town.

Keep a list in your database and refresh it as you go. A great demo, great contacts, and a killer agent along with your work ethic and perseverance will win the day.

How Does a Total Beginner Make These Contacts?

Start by taking a class. That gets you in front of acting teachers. My class is held at a top-notch studio, CRC in Chicago. That gets you in front of engineers and, of course, your teacher. Go to open houses. Take classes where agents participate. Tell your story. Inform others that you are getting into the business. Do dialogue on others' demos—that will get you on the Internet.

The more people who know of your talents, the more opportunities will arise for you. It's a simple numbers game. As the years go on, keep up with those who hire you, reminding them of your latest accomplishments in the business. This growing web of contacts will keep you going during slow periods. A job here or there will do the trick.

If you live in a smaller market, work your area and the area around you. As time passes, work to study in a bigger city—New York, Chicago, or Los Angeles. Chicago is the easiest of the three.

Take some lessons from a local pro to up your game. If you hook up with an agent there, drive in now and again to connect. The effort counts, and they need to see your face. It is great that you can send in material from your home setup to get work, both from a prospective agent and via websites.

Jeff's Advice

Please work with experienced professionals and those who have taught for a while. To make extra income, inexperienced voice actors sometimes take up teaching, and this can create an environment that is not nurturing to your growth. They may inhibit you or be jealous of your abilities. So do an initial session with an experienced, recommended professional. If you like him or her, continue for a few sessions to get good direction and advice.

Early Work

Make sure you update your demo work as time passes and you improve. You don't want to be judged as a newbie when you have done significant work since you last posted a demo. Add new spots and material over time, even if they are just demo pieces.

Review your work periodically to make sure you have quality material representing you.

Social Media

Facebook, LinkedIn, and other sites can offer you platforms to connect with and tell friends and those in the business that you exist and would like their feedback on your work. One thing I learned years ago—and this is true of me, too—is that everyone likes to give his or her opinion, so let this be an initial way to reach future connections and clients.

Be mindful of your content. Drinking shots and getting involved in hot political and religious debates can separate you from those who might want to help you. Act like a pro and you will be treated like one.

ULTIMATE VOICEOVER TIP:

Get into the circle.

A few years ago, I thought about all the jobs I had had since I was a teenager. Every job I got was due to knowing someone at the place of employment. In my entire work life, I have never applied for a job without an inside connection—never. So what does that mean for you?

Getting into the circle means that when you work somewhere—starting as an intern or employee—you should become a person who can be trusted with his or her craft. Preceding a job opportunity, it's all about being with other people—like in a VO class where others get to know you and your vocal talents. If opportunities arise, they will be more apt to recommend you as opposed to a stranger.

This is powerful stuff. The circle concept can apply to any part of your life, work, and play. When you are on the inside, you will get the opportunities over strangers. Give it a shot and enjoy a lifetime of results.

Getting Paid What You Are Worth

I like money. I like getting paid, and I especially like getting paid on time. Most clients fulfill my needs in this capacity. Others delay my gratification.

Most of us come at this business as creative people, actors, improvisers, writers, and musicians. We perform. That is our talent, and the reason we are looking to be in the voiceover business is to use our talent for fun and profit.

Failure to Pay

Let's deal with this up-front here.

Union

If you are a member of SAG-AFTRA, you will merely have your agent report the lateness to the union, and they will handle it. The client will be charged a late fee of around seventy-five dollars or so. You will get this magical check, sometimes months later. I never have not been paid for a job in over thirty years.

Non-union

This is where it can get sticky. We all want to work and work a lot. A client may love us and give us lots of time in the studio, but then when it's time to pay, all we may hear is the clock ticking. This can be hazardous to a freelancer's health and budget.

Up-Front Approaches

- **See if you can be paid at the job, even if at a slight discount.** During election times, you may get cast for a political spot. Definitely ask for the money up-front. After the lost election, the offices close, and the defeated candidate, who may be a lawyer, will not care too much about your paycheck. See the check on the table before you start talking about doing the work.

- **Have your agent call the client.** Be persistent. Keep a visible list of money owed on your computer. You did your job, so now let them do theirs and pay up. Be nice and just say you are checking up on your check. Never be belligerent for any reason. It's counterproductive.

- **Call or e-mail your personal contact for an update.** Again, don't badger because you will want to work with this person again. However, send an e-mail or call every two to three weeks for a follow-up. Be civil, acting as though you know they will pay. Be polite but firm. For example:

  > Hi, Bob. Just checking in on when I might expect payment for...Thanks again for the job. Looking forward to working with you again.

  That works! Part of being a professional is handling your money issues. As creatives, it may be difficult to ask for what you are worth or follow up. You want to be a good guy and not rock the boat.

The Audition

You have done your voiceover training and developed good habits at home. Now is the time to show them off. You have been invited to audition for a commercial that fits your vocal style and range.

Where do auditions come from?

- Your agent.
- Voiceover websites.
- Individual contacts.

If you have an agent, he or she will offer you auditions that fit your particular voice type. This depends on your age, ethnicity, vocal style, versatility, and sex. The more versatile you are, the more auditions you will receive and the more chances you will have to book a job.

If you don't have an agent, you can get an audition on an Internet voiceover site that sends auditions that fit your voice type. You also may have individual contacts who use you outright or have you submit an audition to see if you are the right voice for the job.

All auditions are free. They cost you only your time. If anyone is attaching a fee to this process, stay clear. They are not reputable no matter what they may be offering you.

How Will They Hear You?

- Your agent's website.
- Your website.
- Your audition sent online.
- Your on-air or Internet voice work.

Your agent will send the potential client to either website to hear your voice. If they like you, the audition will take place, and there is the potential for work after that.

If you don't have an agent, Voices.com and Voice123 will connect to your website for voice content.

Once the audition is recorded, the client will hear you on a file with other talent sent from around the country and sometimes the world.

Where Does the Audition Take Place?

Your audition can take place in the following places:

- **The agent's office.** Your agent will have a recording booth in his or her office. An agent will record you at your designated time and put your best takes in a file to be submitted to the client for approval.

- **The casting agent's office or designated studio.** Your casting agent draws talent from all talent agencies, yours being only one of many. The casting agent will have you come into his or her office or, more typically, a designated recording studio to record and submit your audition.

- **The home studio.** In this case, your agent sends you an audition online, and you print up the copy and read on your mike in your home-studio setting. It might just be the microphone at your desk or in your closet, but it is recorded and sent in from home.

How Many Auditions Will I Get in a Given Week?

This really depends on the demand for your style of voice and how many scripts are being auditioned for that style. It also depends on your diversity as a voiceover actor. Do you get auditions across the board (announcer, character, narration, etc.) or are you niched much tighter than this? It also depends on how many voice talents have similar styles at your agency or on your site.

ULTIMATE VOICEOVER TIP!

Get into as many audition circles as possible for better success.

Audition circles are script types that you are right for, such as the following:

- Announcer types.
- Animation character types.
- Narration announcers.
- Promo announcers.
- Audiobook narrators.

As you practice and learn different styles, you will audition across these different circles. Even though you may want to be the next Mel Blanc, Nancy Cartwright, and Billy West all rolled into one, the bulk of your work in most markets is going to be down-the-middle announcer-type roles. These are simple announcer roles or man 1 or 2 in a spot—very basic reads. That is where the bulk of voiceover work is, period. So keep practicing and diversify.

What Goes into a Great Voiceover Audition or Session?

Before you begin your voiceover audition or recording session, here are a few tips for getting you ready to record. Apply these each time you are about to record your audition and each time you are in a session.

Preparation is key to consistency in your reads. It can calm the nerves because of its familiarity and allow the true you to come through in your auditions.

Prerecording Tips

Before a voiceover audition or session, you need to be prepared. The following are some tips to on how to be 100 percent ready to perform:

- **Have something light to eat:**
    - No pasta, dairy products, or anything heavy. You snooze, you lose.
    - Eat nuts, like almonds.
    - Fruits, like apples, are great. Core an apple and put it in a baggie.
    - Bring apple juice.
    - Go easy on caffeine in coffee and colas.
- **Have the right fluids to drink:**
    - Bring apple juice or warm water with a lemon into the studio.
    - Again, go easy on caffeine or your read will get too speedy.
    - Just stay hydrated to keep yourself alert and prevent mouth noise from occurring.
- **Warm up your mouth and mind:**
    - Get in performance mode. Talk with fellow actors and friends.
    - Read the newspaper or do the crossword. Get your mind clicking.
    - Read the script aloud.
    - Do not talk to excess or you will leave your best in the bull pen.
    - Read for five minutes or so just to warm up. No long conversations.
    - Go easy if your voice is a bit hoarse or tired. Drink lots of water.
- **Work scripts immediately:**
    - Study the tone and attitude of the spot (determine, e.g., whether it is upbeat, wry, edgy, etc.).
    - Know how to say the advertiser's name. Say it till it's rote.
    - Mark up your copy.
    - Highlight your part on the script.
    - Underline adjectives and cluster nouns and phrases.

  - Find breaths in scripts if long.
  - Read slowly; gradually speed up, especially on tags.
  - Stay present throughout the script. Finish strong. Run through the tape at the end.

- **Make some choices:**

  - If playing a character, have some different sounds in mind. For example, for the ant for Raid bug spray, you might try deep voices as well as squeaky, scared voices.
  - Name your characters for easy recall.
  - Write the character name or style on the script to remember your choice.
  - Do a natural upbeat read and then become more intimate (up on the mike) or more energetic. Let them know you can brighten or soften your voice.

- **Control your recording space:**

  - Adjust the microphone, copy stand, and microphone volume to comfortable levels.
  - Start talking immediately to gain comfort with your read.

- **Stay flexible and open to direction and new discoveries:**

  - Be willing to try new choices in performance mode.
  - Take a breath. Have fun.

Script Tips

When you get your script to audition, I have a few quick tips to help you get the best out of your reads. Apply these steps repeatedly and you will zone in quickly on the essence of the commercial. I can't promise you will get cast. That is in the ear of the writer who wrote the spot. If you match the voice in the writer's head, you will win the audition. However, if you audition well, you will get more and more opportunities to be the chosen one. Here are things to consider:

- What happened before? What problem are you solving?
- Why was this script created? What is your point and headline?
- Be a storyteller. All commercials are mini stories.
- What is the tone of the spot? Is it conversational, over-the-top, edgy, wry, or something else?
- Mark up the script (look for cluster words, things to underline, etc.).
- Say the product or client's name repeatedly at first for clarity.
- Start slow and build up speed.
- Be deliberate with information, as if you were giving directions.
- Look for repeat words in the commercial.
- Vary your tone to keep the spot interesting.
- Stay present from beginning to end. Run through the tape.

As mentioned previously at greater length, these tips will keep you focused during your audition and session reads.

Read this commercial and then notice how the above list applies:

Weidemark Insurance (pronounced Weed eh Mark)

Trust. It is something you build over time.

Trust is a friend, someone you can count on no matter what.

With trust, all things are possible; limitations fade, and excellence appears.

When you can't trust your insurance carrier to be there for you when trouble hits, you lose the peace of mind a trusted friend brings to your life.

Weidemark Insurance is built on trust, forged by being there for our customers again and again.

For over fifty years, for your home, your auto, your life… Weidemark Insurance is a company you can always count on, a company you can always trust.

Call today and discover the Weidemark difference. 1-800- 655-4400.

What Is the Point?

Weidemark is more trustworthy than other insurance companies.

What Is the Tone?

Conversational and businesslike. Feel free to use your hand to make your point. Lean forward toward the microphone. Be emphatic but use the cell phone read. Don't be loud.

Mark Up Your Script

Here are my markings:

Trust. / It is something / <u>you build</u> / over time.

Trust / is a friend, / someone / <u>you can count on</u> / no matter what.

With **trust**, / all things / are possible; / limitations / fade, / and excellence / appears.

When / you can't **trust /** your <u>insurance carrier</u> / to be there for you / when trouble/ hits,

You lose / <u>the peace of mind</u> / a **trusted** friend / brings to your life.

<u>Weidemark</u> Insurance / is built /on **trust,** / forged / by being there / for our / customers / again and again.

For over <u>fifty years</u>, / for your / home, / your auto, / your life / … <u>Weidemark</u> Insurance / is /a company / you can / always count on, / a company / you can / always trust.

Call today / and discover / the <u>Weidemark</u> difference. / 1-800- / 655- / 4400.

Again, this is just a guide. You can add or subtract markings. Once you break it down and read it a few times, look away from the copy and just roll with it. Don't let the marks make your reading choppy.

Say Client's Name for Clarity

This is job one. It is pronounced *Weed eh Mark.* Say it slowly so you have it and then speed up. Always do this before you even read the spot. Get this out of the way. Ask if you are not sure as to the proper pronunciation and then nail it. If the client is in the session room, you don't want to botch up the name or they might wonder why you were hired.

Start Slow and Build Up Speed

Never come out of the gate too fast. If you can't slow down, do a really slow countdown like I mentioned earlier. Otherwise the read will get too fast and you will make mistakes (slurred words, misspeaking, etc.). Start slow and naturally build up speed that comes with script familiarity.

Be Deliberate with Information

Like a tour guide through the commercial, methodically land on each copy point and be definitive with your statements. Keep moving at the right speed but think of each copy point of information as a stepping stone—go one at a time till the spot is complete.

Look for Repeat Words in the Commercial or Copy

Before even reading a piece of copy, note whether there are repeat words that are used as a theme in the copy. In this case it is the word *trust*. This repeat word should be emphasized differently with each reading. Your options are to apply an up, medium, or down inflection.

Vary Your Tone to Make the Script Interesting

ULTIMATE VOICEOVER TIP!

Observe the two-line rule.

Usually after reading two lines of dialogue, you need to change the pace to keep the script interesting.

You can be fast, slow, high, medium, low, in on the microphone, and off the microphone. If you simply jump into the two words *with truth* in the script above a bit more quickly, you will effect change in your copy.

In general, the more you plot out your changes or simply do them naturally, the more interesting and effective your read will be. Your job as a reader is to keep the listener engaged in your read. Contrast is the key here. Slowing down, speeding up, and moving up on and back off of your mike will make this happen. Change speeds and the mike position even in a single long written line as well.

Stay Present from Beginning to End and Run through the Tape

Work to stay present for each copy point you deliver. This is achieved by being deliberate with your information, landing on the words. It's like serving an hors d'oeuvre at a party: make contact and pass it out. Of course, you will do pickups to cover copy you didn't read cleanly. That's fine. But work to make sure you stay present for each copy point of your story. Remember you are building a story, even if it is only fifteen, thirty, or sixty seconds long.

So...Did I Get the Spot?

You audition. Actually, you audition a lot. You go to your agents or record at home. You did a great audition. You sent it in, and now you are waiting to hear if you are cast.

How long do you have to wait?

Well, that varies. Sometimes the client has a quick record date mentioned on the audition specs. Many times your audition goes into the ether, never to be seen or heard of again. Why?

- **Someone else was cast.** Rats. It happens all the time. Get used to it. Your job is to follow the specs for the spot or voiceover and supply a great read. They decide if your voice fits the sound they require. I call TV the Blown Auditions channel. Seeing your spot on TV with someone else's voice can be depressing. This is like seeing another guy driving your girlfriend's or boyfriend's car. Uh-oh.

- **The voiceover project or script was killed.** The project could have been on shaky ground at the audition stage. Perhaps it didn't meet full client needs, or a simple change of mind occurred. Either way, your audition is toast.

- **The voiceover project was delayed.** Perhaps they loved your voice but the script needed some adjustments. This stalls the project, and you will hear nothing. This is frustrating, especially if you feel you nailed it. I have had producers tell me I am going to do a spot and then do it almost a year later (this happened to me with Raid). This is unusual, but it can happen.

- **Your audition is being played as free demo for the client.** This can happen very easily. Your great audition might get played in the conference room for the client. If they like it, perhaps they will call you to do the final session for the air. If not, they may have played your audition and went another way with the project. They should pay you for this, and they do many times—but other times they do not. Don't have a cow. You won't know about this anyway unless you have someone on the inside. Forget about it.

I would say that for most projects you should know in one or two weeks. If the cell phone flashes with your agent's name up top, it could be good news. If not…

ULTIMATE VOICEOVER TIP!

Keep your auditions in the rearview mirror.

Once you have auditioned, forget about it. Look up ahead. Let the audition fade from memory. If not, you will wondering and bothering your agent and causing undo mental concern for yourself. Believe me, if they want you, the phone will ring. Every once in a while, you'll have a callback, but this is hardly the norm for the VO business. Traditionally, you will audition and then hear back or not. So just keep sending out great auditions, and your time will come.

The Voiceover Session

Congratulations! You have been hired. Out of all the auditions, the client and the advertising agency liked yours the best. That is amazing. You will now do one of the following:

- Report to a recording studio to record your commercials or VO project.
- Record at home in your studio if you were cast agent-free through a website.

The following will deal with recording at a recording studio.

Your preparation will be the same as described above in the "Prerecording Tips" section.

- **Above all, be early to your job.** Let the client know you are there and ready to go. You don't want them calling your agent to find out where you were. Plan where to park if driving. Know your location ahead of time.

- **Have a pencil and highlighter to mark copy.** Prep your copy before stepping in front of microphone. This prevents mistakes and makes you look like a pro.

- **Keep a low profile in the session. Focus on your work, not on opinions or personal business.** Always remember, you are entering a professional setting at a recording. Even though the creative team might be young like you, be courteous and professional. Keep your talking for in front of the microphone. Greet everyone and then get to work on your script. Don't let loose language sink your ship. You never know who is listening on the line. All it takes is one offended person on the client side to hear you drop an f-bomb for you to become persona non grata.

Secondly, don't talk shopping excursions or expensive vacations, flaunting how you have all this money and free time to spend it. VO work is part-time, and others work full-time and don't come and go all day like we do. A lot of them feel we are lucky, spoiled, or both. So keep things to a minimum. Be deferential. Keep your exciting trip to Borneo to your friends and family.

- **Stay open to direction.** You are a puppet in front of the microphone, and your puppeteer is on the other side of the glass. The writer knows what he wants to hear and will direct you to that elusive sound in his head. Go where he or she leads you and deliver the sound he or she wants. Remember to put your brain in a box. Move like one of those old rabbit-ear antennae covered with tinfoil—left, right, up, and down—till you get there.

ULTIMATE VOICEOVER TIP!

Don't verbalize your ideas in front of the microphone. It is always the creative team's idea.

Read the copy and let the writer discover it. If you telegraph your idea by saying, "Hey, I have this different way to read it," the creative staff will go on guard and not hear it with unbiased ears. I found this to be the kiss of death for me. So I would merely read it a bit differently and then hear the approval (usually) afterward. Then—and here is the important part—it becomes their idea. When it is their idea, they love it usually. This is strange but true.

- **Make copy changes cleanly.** Things can get hot and heavy in front of the microphone. Copy will be changed, and sentences and copy points will be eliminated. Make sure you totally cover up changed copy so your eye doesn't trip on it going through the read.

- **Look away from the copy stand and clear your mind after a few reads.** It is really easy to become myopic or too focused on your copy, You start reading it instead of merely reacting to what is written. This is how you communicate in real life, not so conscious of the sound of our own voice and how you say each syllable or word. Stare at the floor, look to your left or right, and come back for the next take with a fresh mind. You will have absorbed the directions from the creatives. If you missed it, you will pick it up next time.

ULTIMATE VOICEOVER TIP!

After the client approves your read, do one more full take before you go.

Unless the client or creative team says no, try one more full read of the VO copy. This applies to short (fifteen-, thirty-, or sixty-second) commercial reads. Why? I feel that after receiving approval I always relaxed and would read even better. Many times the read I gave after all the work on the spot delivered the result that went on the air. Don't act like what you did was unsatisfactory—the client liked it. Just go one step further to give them an even better read than before.

- **At conclusion, thank all in the room and get their business cards or names on the script.** These folks had the good taste to hire you. You want to keep up with them by entering their names in your database. Staying connected is essential for long-term success in any business. Send the creatives a thank you via card or e-mail. It will show your gratitude, which is a powerful tool in getting hired again—perhaps without an audition the next time.

- **Get permission from the client or creative staff to get a copy of your work.** In the exciting afterglow of your tremendous performance in-session, it is time to ask to get a copy of your work. This work will be added at a future date to your demo reel to show off your talents to future employers. If you wait, you may have to make additional phone calls back and forth, and that is a drag. A good engineer, with approval, should be able to burn you a CD right on the spot. You want the larger file or WAVE file for better fidelity on your demo reel. An MP3 may sound OK, but go for the original file format.

Marketing: Branding Yourself in the Voiceover Business

One of the fun things about the voiceover business is that you're a one-man or -woman band. You are not only an actor delivering a great read but also a marketer of your talents and your brand in this business. I found it fun to come up with marketing and promotional ideas for myself to heighten others' awareness of me. However, I do advocate enlisting professionals in each category of recording and visual design to put your work on a level with others in the business. Appearance counts.

Lets start with your voiceover demo.
Your voiceover demo represents you and your vocal talents. Your demo reel is your verbal diploma. Like a medical or law degree, your demo reel establishes your authenticity in the business. As a demo producer, I feel it is vital to have a professional-sounding sample of your work. Here are some basic tips to get you started on this process:

DEMO TIPS

- One minute is all you need.
- Avoid high-priced demo packages.
- Create a commercial voiceover demo first.
- Find on-air spots that sound like you.
- Listen to talent on websites for samples.
- Find an engineer who produces spots to record you.

- Find a great coach or writer to create material for you.
- Create a visual that captures your voice style.
- Get feedback from agents before making copies.
- Present demo on CD and MP3 formats.

One Minute Is All You Need

Just give the client a taste of what you offer. If it's too long, you'll overstay your welcome. The first three takes should be your winners—your best work. Show contrast in the first three takes.

Avoid High-Priced and Low-Priced Demo Packages

Demo packages come in all shapes and sizes. If it is too cheap—$500 to $900—you may receive the following results:

- Poor music choices.
- Stale, overused copy.
- Lack of variety due to poor direction.
- A need to redo the demo reel later, costing more money.
- No protection from music licensing fees (see Tune-Sat, page 233-4).

If it is too expensive—$3,500 to $5,000—you may receive the following results:

- Overworked copy.
- Too many takes, making you look ready when you are not.
- Too many unnecessary lessons.
- An inability to allocate funds to other necessary spending (e.g., on a website).
- False promises of work connections.

Why Can't I Just Do My Own Demo?

You have the recording equipment. You have previously produced spots. You know how to master and edit digital audio. So why not save money and cut your own demo?

In this case, you can. If merely stacking up produced spots is your aim and you have the abilities listed above, give it a shot. However, have someone else listen to judge its length, variety, and individual castable selections.

Jeff's Advice

Producing your own demo is like cutting your own hair.

I have been in the business for over thirty years. I would never, ever, ever do my own demo. Why?

- Lack of objectivity ("I love that clown spot"…uh, no).
- Inability to direct to a different read if necessary.
- Amateur engineering skills.
- Not using broadcast quality spots (perhaps your W. C. Fields impression is not good).

Follow the mastermind theory. Use quality masters all along the way: engineers, copywriters, webmasters, and others. The combined energy and synergy will raise you to the top.

Create a Commercial Voiceover Demo First

This is the place to start. A great commercial demo consists of the following:

Cut 1: Just you talking in a relaxed, conversational mode.
Cut 2: Contrast to cut one. Deeper, raspier, or sexier.
Cut 3: Solid track. Bull's-eye read differently from one and two. Signature read.
(if they stopped here, they would know your sound).
Cut 4: Quick dialogue.
Cut 5: Short character piece.
Cut 6: Announcer track. Something that hasn't been heard before and is a contrast to the above.
Cut 7: Repeat of bull's-eye sound (deep, folksy, etc.) but with a twist (e.g., conversational going into an accent). Double voice spot.
Cut 8: Finish strong with a great ending.

This is just one template, but it can serve you well if executed. You may have more than eight tracks, but keep in mind we are shooting for around one minute of recording.

Though you may excel at doing animated characters, audiobooks, or narration, your agent needs to hear you in the commercial realm first with basic conversational and stylized announcers and a few character and dialogue pieces to round it out.

You can then do other demos for your specialty, whether that is characters, animation, narration, audiobooks, promos, or something else.

Find On-Air Spots That Sound Like You

Advertising is a copycat business. Certain vocal styles stay popular over the long run, and other flavor-of-the-month styles come in and out.

- Long-term sounds: Folksy, gritty, big voice of God, nasally, and honest and straight.
- Flavors: Popular celebrity sounds. I can remember when they wanted a "Bruce Willis sound." It might be Denis Leary now.

Simply, what is on the air has been cast, and covering that sound will help you in auditions. Don't try to be all things—just what suits your vocal style.

Listen to Talent on Websites for Samples

Know who you are up against. Sampling top-notch talent shows you the quality that gets hired over and over. Again, cover the sounds you hear that fit your voice. Check major agencies in Chicago, Los Angeles, and New York. The sounds will amaze you. Don't be intimidated. You can do amazing work with practice, good scripts, and engineering.

Find an Engineer who Produces Spots to Record You

This is crucial to producing a great demo. Musician friends, self-taught home engineers, and others can record you, but an engineer who produces on-air commercials every day is the way to go. He or she will know all the nuances, music choices, and more to make your demo sound like it was edited from on-air material. People who listen to your demo should be able to say, "Did you do that spot? Sounds great!"

Your demo should have top-notch produced pieces that can be used for years. The up-front cost may be a bit more, but not having to produce an entirely different demo after a year or so saves you money in the long run.

ULTIMATE VOICEOVER TIP!

Be careful what music you use on your demo.

In the past, since demos are not for broadcast, the law was flexible about what music was allowed to be included in them. However, with the spread of Internet play, placement companies like Tune-Sat are monitoring content with the purpose of retrieving fees for music clients who are not getting paid for their work.

Tune-Sat's unique audio fingerprint technology monitors hundreds of TV channels and millions of websites around the world, helping rights holders collect millions of dollars that would otherwise have been lost.

Find a Great Coach or Writer to Create Material for You

Many cheaper demo producers just give you a pile of scripts and have you record. A great combo of coach and writer tailors material to you and rewrites or creates original material that suits your voice.

ULTIMATE VOICEOVER TIP!

Get an advertising copywriter to supply or write scripts.

Every ad writer has a stack of scripts that did not make it to air. He or she would love to hear a fine voice like yours on a spot and to hear his or her great fallen idea finally produced. I did this in my early days. The scripts are fun and fresh and can add a lot to your demo. Ask around. Maybe a friend works at an agency. See what you can accomplish. It is worth it.

Create a Visual That Captures Your Voice Style

Simplicity is everything here. First off, don't use your head shot if you have one. You don't want to have yourself typecast by your individual look. A caricature of your flowing red hair or your general look is fine, but do not use any actual photos—just something that gives us the essence of what you are personality wise. Go for a simple font or logo that captures your personality. This image can be used for:

- A demo cover.
- Business cards.
- Writing pads.

- Website home page.
- Social media profile shots (Facebook, Twitter, LinkedIn, etc.).

ULTIMATE VOICEOVER TIP!

Take your visual and tack it to the wall across the room.

Now forget it's there. Come back in at a later time and see if it pops out at you. Can you read it clearly? Is it too busy? Do the colors meld together? A simple, clear logo impregnates itself into prospective clients' minds. Don't get cute or too fancy. Simple is best.

Get Feedback from Agents before Making Copies

Ah, yes, feedback. That is a powerful word. It enables future agents or clients to review your work without the need to decide whether to hire or represent you on the spot. It is a simple effective way to create a new creative relationship. An agent's feedback is vital to how he or she can niche you in the business and put you on the right road for voiceover work. When I produce a demo with my partner David Leffel at BAM Studios, we are only two-thirds of the important voices needed. The agent's voice is vital to round out what you have on your demo. His or her comments will zone in your demo to make it more effective.

ULTIMATE VOICEOVER TIP!

Be careful of who gives you feedback on your demo.

Friends and family can over compliment or dismiss your work. Neither type of comment matters. If they are not in the profession, you should avoid allowing their thoughts to impact your work. I have seen female clients have their boyfriends not even listen to their work. That's nothing to worry about. Your boyfriend—thank God—is not hiring you. Get feedback from those in the business, such as

- Agents.
- Fellow VO artists.
- Copywriters.
- Ad producers and directors.
- Engineers.

These are the only folks who can help you get legitimate feedback. Hear the overall comments, and if a tweak or two is needed to be done on your work, do it.

Present Your Demo in CD and MP3 Formats

You want to have a hard copy that shows your visual and presents your audio on CD. This has a continued presence when given to a prospective agent. It sits on the desk waiting to be listened to when needed. An MP3—a compressed version of your original WAVE or AIFF file—arrives in seconds, but as the screen refreshes at your future agent's office, you get swept away. So present both. The CD format makes you feel like you really accomplished something, which you have. The MP3 is better for instant listening if clients want to hear you now and don't have a hard copy.

ULTIMATE VOICEOVER TIP!

Make sure your contact information is easy to read on the CD and cover.

Duh, right? But you would be surprised by how many talent have their contact info (name, phone number, agent, and e-mail address) on the CD cover and not on the CD. OK, so maybe they listen to you. They like you. So they look at the CD. There's no number. Where is the cover? It's upstairs somewhere at the agency. Don't make it hard for them to contact you. Don't get cute with your artwork. Just give them the facts, and all will be well.

The Website

One of the most important next steps once you have your demo completed is to create a website for yourself. You don't need it right away, but if you can produce this in tandem with your visual look, you will be ahead of the action.

Websites can be self-created (use web.com, intuit.com, etc.) for little or no cost. Others will hire a website producer to handle this chore. I believe in letting each expert in the line (engineers, visual artists, website producers) do his or her thing. They are the experts and can offer great artistry that will affect how you are heard and received. It's more expense, but your website may not have the professional look that says you are a professional otherwise. I feel very strongly about this.

Components of a website include the following:

- A simple home page visual.
- Simple buttons to access your demo or demos.
- A simple contact button to reach you and your future agent.

ULTIMATE VOICEOVER TIP!

Have separate contact buttons for each acting talent.

One website is enough, but have separate buttons to access voiceover and on-camera content. When they hit *voiceover*, they should get your audio content. When they hit *on-camera*, they should get your TV and film content. They should be able to see your head shot here but not on your home page.

Make your home page visually friendly—not busy, but simple and easy on the eyes. You should not be judged by your graphics but by your voiceover abilities. Focus on your strengths. There's no need to list every job you have ever had on the site. It will come off like you are a jack-of-all-trades and master of none.

Once your website is completed, you can do the following:

- Link to it from your agent's website.
- Link to it from audition sites: Voices.com, Voice123, Voicebank.
- Link to it from production studios, including local recording studios.

But be mindful of posting your demo on sites other than your website.

The good thing about your website is that you can post a variety of voiceover content on it, including all of the following:

- A commercial demo.
- A narration demo.
- A promo demo.
- A character and animation demo.
- A gaming demo.
- An audiobook demo.

In addition, if you want to put longer content not suitable for your commercial demo (e.g., full commercials, dialogues with others, dialogues with your individual characters), it can be posted, too. Anyone who visits your website can dive in anywhere he or she wants. If you have enough material to allow for an extended stay, so be it, but remember to make it easy for visitors to access your work.

Social Media

Social media functions in a variety of different ways, but these are the top three:

- **With Facebook,** you can share your overall thoughts and lifestyle with as much (or as little) family, friends, and business connections as you want. Obviously it can be lighthearted and upbeat or politically corrosive depending on your individual bent. Be mindful of your picture content. Showing yourself as a party lush may not work for your overall business image. Sharing your latest on-air spot on YouTube shows that you are kicking it in the VO biz. Just try not to brag too much. Fellow VO talent would love to be on the upper ladder step with you. You can also show other interesting talents of yours, like painting skills or musical skills. But remember to hone in on your best skill set and never let them forget you are great at that.

- **With Twitter,** you tend to offer random comments and opinions in reaction to ongoing events. Make sure you think twice before overreacting to an event and firing off a tweet that shows you off in a negative way. I'd be real really careful on this one.

- **With LinkedIn,** you are received on a professional level. Your hirable skills are on display. Again, put your VO skills up front and reveal other talents below. Again, there's no need to post everything you ever did in your life. Keep it focused.

There are plenty others besides these, such as Tumblr, which is more full-content friendly. You can be involved in social media across the board, but the above three are the leaders in the clubhouse at present.

Social media sites come and go with certain ones holding sway as the most commonly used. The top three seem to be best at the time of this book's writing. These should be at the top for a while, but try to keep up with trends by consulting with younger folk and people in the social media industry. Things change fast these days.

ULTIMATE VOICEOVER TIP!

People usually remember you for one talent.

You may have creative skills in a variety of areas, but if you want to be a voiceover artist, focus your attention there. Let prospective clients and agents know you are honing this craft so they will think of you highly. Sure, as an actor you will be cast in other formats, such as TV, film, and stage. That is all well and good. However, share your other abilities—in music, art, and other crafts—with those of like or similar skill sets. Those folks will see you as the cool musician, painter, woodworker, or whatever.

My career took off when I focused on VO. As I moved into teaching, my body of work set me up to teach locally and at the college level. Acting School of Chicago and Columbia College see me as a top-notch VO talent who is now sharing his experience. I do other things, such as writing and spoken-word comedy, but I am seen, by fellow students, and VO talent as a VO guy. I am proud to be a VO lifer.

Giveaways

This may be an old-school method of reaching clients or rewarding them. However, it is effective and fun. The Chicago school of VO was very steeped in giving away the following:

- Pens.
- Pads (writing pads, not I-Pads, although maybe for big clients).
- Postcards.
- Cups.
- Calendars.
- Post-it notes.
- Coasters.
- Refrigerator magnets.

Your logo can be displayed on all these items except for pens, which require simple graphics. They stay on clients' desks and in studios. My "have a cup on Jeff" ceramic coaster stayed in studios for years and years, keeping wooden consoles clear of cup rings. It is a simple way to say thank-you and keep your name floating around agencies and studios. Lots of times when you get your CD completed, promotion or fulfillment companies will offer you a matching pad to go with the CD design. It's not a bad idea to take it.

In my time I did all of the above. Postcards tend to get tossed pretty quickly, so I would be careful about that. Giving something directly to a client is a better idea. It's funny how corny a calendar may seem, but don't we always need one at the first of the year?

ULTIMATE VOICEOVER TIP!

Find a promotion that fits your own personality.

When I began my career, I was not comfortable promoting myself unless I had found an idea that was more than just a way of pleading with people to remember me. I did a pad with my face on it that read "Draw on Jeff." Clients poked out my eyes, put on weird mustaches, and more. They sent them back to me in an early example of interactive advertising. This is still remembered today. Another talent had a chattering teeth windup toy for his Tag Man logo. This was silly but fun. Find something that works for you. Have fun with it.

PART V: Getting Hired

SUMMARY

- Get voiceover work from a variety of sources.
- Decide whether union or nonunion work is best for you.
- Establish and maintain contacts in the business.
- Get paid what you are worth.
- Be prepared to record.
- Know how to brand yourself.

PART VI
Getting Better

Tricks, Tips, and Troubleshooting

The point of this section is to give you quick reminders, shortcuts, and tips to review before you go into an audition or session. I need to remind myself of these basics even at this late date.

This book holds a lot of info. This section will be a sort of review of some of the concepts I introduced in the many pages before this. There might be some repetition in this section, but we do forget a lot of what we first hear, so impregnating the info helps it to stick in our minds. Think of this a Fourth of July fireworks finale. Enjoy.

Ultimate Voiceover Express:
Seven Steps to VO Greatness

1. Read out loud…a lot. Read all kinds of copy in different ways. To be a great reader, you have to read out loud a lot. Learn the tone of the spot so you can return to it next audition. Don't ever over read or memorize.

2. Soak in the sounds and engage in voice immersion. Listen and copy all kinds of voice types. Put on your headsets and let your brain soak in different type of voices, accents, dialects, impressions, and animated characters. Learn seasonal sounds like elves for Christmas and spooky voices for Halloween. Learn stock voices like game show hosts, auctioneers, big movie promo guys, Gypsy fortune-tellers, and sports announcers. Go online and have a feast.

3. Learn the business from an experienced professional. Let him or her zone in your talents and expand your repertoire. It is worth the time and money for the right person. The key term here is *experienced professional*. Many times you will encounter voiceover talent who have very little experience teaching what they themselves have not mastered. Stick with the highly experienced professionals. You will not be disappointed.

4. Be eligible for multiple audition circles. Learn and master the art of straight commercial announcing styles, characters, animated characters, narration reads, and promos. Keep learning new styles to up your repertoire. But harness what you do best.

5. Create and nurture your business contacts. Even more important than an agent are the people who will hire you. Guard them like precious jewels. They will remember you and hire you again and again. Keep in touch. You won't regret it!

6. Keep investing in your talents. Invest in ways to promote yourself. Build a website and invest in equipment for daily practice and to send in your auditions from home.

7. Take care of yourself, mentally, physically, and spiritually. Invest time and energy into knowing your true self. The more balanced you are as a person, the better you will do in the business. Enjoy life and let voiceover be a positive part of it.

ULTIMATE VOICEOVER TIP!

Take good care of your voice.

Keep your ax sharpened 24-7. Be mindful of how you are feeling and how your voice is doing. Stay away from dairy if a cold is coming on. Use steam, hot water with lemon, and at times, rest your voice to prevent further issues. Do not yell. If you feel yourself coughing from straining a bit, stop. Warm up with basic conversation in person or on the phone. Don't make it anything too heavy. Bring apple juice or apple slices to the session to cut mouth noise. Just be mindful overall.

Psychology of the Business

So much of success in the voiceover business has to do with your mind-set:

- Do you think positively or negatively?
- Do you believe that you can succeed in this business?
- Do you work hard to achieve your goals?
- Do you get down if VO work slows down?
- Do you stop or keep going when adversity hits?

Before we get into the nuts and bolts of getting hired, let's talk about the power of our mind and thoughts to create good for us in this business. I bring this up here because I feel this is a powerful shortcut and I would be remiss not to mention it again as a vital part of my success in voiceover. It's a challenging path, but nonetheless, a healthier option than constantly fighting with yourself and ultimately your own good.

My Story

As a kid, I was an audio sponge, imitating anything I heard on TV and in the movies. Impressions came free and easy. I narrated my own pickup basketball games with my nonstop sports-announcer chatter.

In college at Northwestern University, I got my comedy and voice training as a DJ at our student station, WNUR-AM, where I broadcasted my own jazz blues show, a sports program, and an original comedy show with playwright Keith Reddin called *Perverts on Parade*, featuring plenty of crazy voices. In addition, I opened my creative floodgates by performing for three years in *The Mee-Ow Show*, an original improvisational review.

However, upon graduation, I lacked a sufficient comfort level with performance. I had a cocky confidence in my voice abilities, but my mental approach was wrong. I did not like performing for strangers; instead I clammed up and became combative, which was not a great combination for success.

As I mentioned earlier in this book, my competitive nature got the best of me and made me way too intense. This intensity hampered the easy flow of my creative vocal talents. Simply, I was way too hard on myself and needed to relax in this new environment.

Luckily, my first agent Pamela Jefferson of Jefferson and Ellis believed in me, telling me that I could be a six-figure talent someday soon. I believed her because she had others in her stable who had achieved that and more.

It didn't happen right away, yet I knew it would happen because she had planted the seed and I let it grow. The simple belief that I could achieve a high level of income drove me—that and the fact that I had just started a family and wanted to be able to support my two children, Zach and Lila, and give them a great life.

How the Heck Did This Happen? Number One: I Needed a New Mind-Set.

I immersed myself in self-help reading, focusing on positive thinking. I listened to tapes to impregnate new thoughts of plenty and destroy negative thoughts of lack. Reverend Catherine Ponder's prosperity readings helped me maintain a positive edge and be diligent to eliminate negative thoughts about the voiceover business. Dr. Joseph Murphy taught me about dropping positive thoughts into the subconscious mind.

Let's face it: even when on a roll, we are still not selected for most of our auditions. It takes daily diligence to not let old harmful thoughts grow and impede our progress. I've always felt it was like cleaning a table before eating—making sure it is wiped down and not full of clutter before having a meal. It transformed my life.

Give this some thought. Wearing handcuffs on that powerful mind of yours is no way to fly. Believe in yourself by practicing belief. I like to say "I am doing a great audition [or session] today." Feel it. See it. Let it make you smile.

See great results and expect the best. Trust you must. I always point out the process of mailing a letter as a powerful example of trust in our lives. We put a valuable message or check in an envelope and put it in a metal box. A man with a leather bag takes our letter, walks around the neighborhood, and eventually deposits our letter in a pile to be sorted at the post office. Rapidly the letters, ours included, get sorted. It then gets on a plane in a bag and arrives where we had indicated it to be sent, and it is sorted and given to another man with a leather bag. Somehow, in time, our letter arrives almost 100 percent of time. We totally believe this will happen. So apply this simple faith to your life and believe that you can train yourself and be successful. It sure beats the alternative.

Let Your Body Do the Talking:
How Body Language Can Affect Reading

When you are standing in front of a microphone, let your body help you do the talking. Even though your mouth is doing all the heavy lifting, how you use the rest of your body can help your read. "OK, Jeff," you might say. "What the heck are you talking about?"

For instance, for aggressive-sounding reads (Midas Brakes or Chevy Trucks—real manly reads), lean forward and point your finger when talking. This is an aggressive posture—how you would act if you wanted to be strong in communicating a point in a real-life conversation—no sense changing that natural body posture when doing a commercial. In fact, imitating the body language will make your read more genuine. Next, for a laid-back, relaxed read, just put your hands in your pockets and rock a bit on your heels. This is a more passive posture used for easygoing conversational reads. Doing this posture will kill all the push in your read.

Let's say you want a distracted, somewhat airheaded read (e.g., a forgetful husband or girl friend). You should move away so that the script is out of sight and then move back when you are about to read. If you want to sound genuinely distracted, be distracted. Your body language speaks volumes, and it will in front of the microphone as well. As casting agent David Lewis of Chicago always says, move those arms around.

Mental Block Alert

Ah, yes, the mental block. They are so much fun to have in a recording session. You get to a word or phrase, and no matter how much you try, you keep saying the word or phrase the wrong way. You may also emphasize the wrong part of the word or syllable, or you may go up in inflection instead of down or down instead of up. What should you do?

As a novice, I would speed up to immediately to hide my mistake. This was the wrong way to go. I would keep trying it the same way, making the same mistake and just getting more and more frustrated, wanting to pull my faulty brain out my head.

When time is money and you are in front of the advertising creative team, you want to do your best, and beating up on yourself accomplishes nothing.. You waste time and energy.

So I developed the following steps to help me (and now you) when the proverbial poop hits the fan. All will be well if you don't think but just react differently. Stuff happens, and it's your reaction that can save or sink you in-session.

First: Slow Down

Say the troublesome word or phrase super slowly so you have it. Then speed up again.

Second: Say It in a Different Way

Speed up or slow down the problem word or phrase so your brain gets out of its rut.

Third: Insert a Different Adjective or a Color.

Take the word "summertime." Let's say you are emphasizing the *time* instead of the *summer*. Insert a color, like so:

Blue time
Red time
Summer time.

Fourth: Spell Out the Word Differently

Take the word *integral*. In big letters write *INTA GRUL* or whatever it takes for your mind to get it.

Don't ask why. Don't fight your brain. You will lose. Just change it up, mostly by slowing down to get the word or phrase you want. Then, speed up. Do the above, and you will solve your problems easily.

Troubleshooting Tricks

Many times in a session or audition, you run up against certain issues that can bring you down and ruin your read. I offer here tried-and-true techniques that have helped me immeasurably over my long and illustrious career (ha-ha).

Problem: Choppy first paragraphs for narrations
Solution: The narration "read around"

Read the last paragraph and then read the first paragraph again.
The first paragraph of a narration can be a mishmash of direction reminiscent of Frankenstein's monster. You will get a ton of initial direction to get you zoned in on that first page. As you progress through the read, you will start flowing and no longer need the same amount of direction. So read the first paragraph after the last to give a fresh "in the flow" feel.

Problem: Annoying *p* pops
Solution: Talk across or under the microphone

It's very common to get a "popping *p*" sound on the mike when recording. This problem is caused by throwing too much breath at the microphone. Here are some easy solutions to this vexing problem:

Old School

1. Tap your mouth with your forefinger when you say the *p* word. It pops the bubble of sound that hits the microphone too hard.

2. Turn your head slightly to the right when the *p* word appears. This will send the breath away from the mike.

New School

1. Talk across the microphone. Just slant your read to the left or right a little. Your voice will be heard, but the plosive sound of the *p* will not.

2. Dip your head just below the mike on the *p* words, sending the dreaded plosive sound downward.

I usually use option one under "New School" because I position myself so this problem is eliminated right from the start.

Do not adjust the microphone yourself in a studio setting. It would be so easy to just grab that mike and yank it down to where you want it to be. Don't. Think of any studio microphone as red-hot—too hot to touch. Studio microphones are the best and very expensive. Always ask the engineer to adjust it for you before starting your session. Working in a heavy union town like Chicago, if you even look at the microphone funny, an aggressive union guy might take you down. That is their job. You do yours. Speak but don't touch.

Problem: Reading too fast.
Solution: Slow "3," "2," "1" countdown.

It's important to start slow in your reads. Like when meeting someone for the first time, you should begin with a slow introduction. Your first line is to ground you in the read—to set the pace for increasing the speed for the rest of the read.

If you start too fast, you may slip and slide through the rest of the copy. It's like running on ice too fast: you will most likely slip and fall. That said, the solution when you are reading too fast, is to anchor your read with a slow countdown to get you started properly.

Count out "3 (beat) 2 (beat) 1 (beat)," and you will start slower. Give it a try.

Problem: Reading too slowly.
Solution: Compress your breath to better maximize the speed of your read.

Put your tongue at the roof of your mouth and make a quick "da da da da da" sound. From this mouth position, shoot your breath in a compressed manner to maximize it and get through copy more quickly. This method reduces the amount of inhaling and exhaling to cut the read time significantly.

Problem: Choppy, staccato read.
Solution: Exhale the copy.

If you are being asked to "smooth it out" by your creative team, simply take a deep breath and exhale out your copy. It will have a smoother sound. I challenge you to read choppy when you simply exhale your copy.

The Voice Accordion

Creating character or animation voices:

The point of this exercise is to take your voice and exaggerate it for the purposes of creating a character or animation voice. It occurred to me as I was teaching my Voice for Animation class at Columbia College in

Chicago that if you merely exaggerate your own voice through speed changes—like by moving your voice in and out like an accordion—you can create new voices to play with up and down your register. Let's try this out.

1. **Make a sound.**

2. **Talk through sound with copy.** "Hey, it's me, [name of your character], your new voice friend. I am looking to do a lot of work for you in commercials, TV, and movies. I can really do all kinds of things, like…"

3. **Talk slow.** "I'm talking reallllly slow. As slow…as I…possibly can. Realllly, reallllly slooooow."

4. **Talk faster.** "Then I speed up a bit and talk faster. This way I can say more things, and you can hear my voice in a different way."

5. **Talk even faster.** "And now I am talking really, really, really fast, so fast I barely know what I'm saying. It's like I drank a pot of coffee or a gallon of Red Bull, and the words keep flying out of my mouth over and over and over and over and over and over again. Oh boy! Ahh!"

6. **Talk slower.** "Whew, well, this is much better. Still kinda fast but not so fast I can't catch my breath. I much prefer this, but…"

7. **Talk even slower.** "And nowwww I am baaack in slooooow motion. This…is…weird."

8. **Do your regular voice.** "Well, that was fun. Think of me when you cast your next voice!"

Speaking Styles Exercise

- **Chewing the words:** High emphasis, deliberate landing, and sticking on words and phrases.

- **Voice trigger:** Act like you are chewing slowly like a cow.

Samples

- The all new Ford F-150. Built strong and priced to ride. Stop by your Ford dealer today for a test drive.
- Delicious barbecue ribs, slathered in sauce and cooked to perfection

  - **Matter-of-fact:** Shoulder-shrug, hands-in-pocket read.
  - **Excited:** Voice trigger: wow!
  - **Aggressive:** Trigger. Finger point and lean in on mike.
  - **Talk over noise:** Quiet yell over outdoor noise.
  - **Internal dialogue:** Talk outside of your mouth—a quiet, echoey sound.

Voiceover Potholes and How to Fix Them

- **Slow it down.** Do a countdown and then read.
- **Cleaner copy points.** Do a slow alphabet countdown: "A (beat) B (beat) C (beat)" and then read the copy.
- **Smooth it out.** Take a breath in and then breathe out the copy.
- **Speed it up.** Compress your breath and put your tongue to the top of your mouth. Make the noise "da da da da da" like Jack Webb from *Dragnet*.
- **Clip the read.** To prevent mushy sounding copy reads, jab your finger in the air. This makes your read crisper and also gets rid of regional accents.

- **Vary the read.** Do a character cleanse. Read the copy with a silly character voice and return. Also, boot the brain. Look at the floor for a few seconds and then read the copy.
- **Not so announcery.** Take off your headset and act like you are talking on cell phone. Then read the copy again.
- **Not so aggressive.** Put your hands in your pockets and lean back on your heels.
- **More friendly.** Just smile and then talk through your smile.
- **More forceful.** Lean forward and poke your finger when you talk.
- **Stuck on a word.** Break it up into syllables. Replace word you are especially stuck on with a color adjective. Let's say you can't say the phrase *marking time* without goofing up the word *marking*. Take out *marking* and insert a color—*blue*, perhaps. Say "blue time, red time, marking time." Sneak it in there and fool the brain. Don't worry why you are doing it this way. Just change and get your car back on the road.
- **Kill those popping *p* words.** Speak across the mike or just under it.
- **Create a new character.** Make a sound, support it, and speak through it.

PART VI: Getting Better

SUMMARY

- Know the psychology of the business.
- Observe your script checklist before recording.
- Use your body when communicating on the mike.
- Observe troubleshooting tips.
- Be a voice accordion.
- Fix your VO potholes for better reads.
- Enjoy the VO business.

Finale: Thanks for reading and good luck!

Whew. We have made it to the end. If you have read this book in its entirety, you have taken in a lot of information, techniques, and tips to help you learn and eventually master the voiceover business. Remember, I learned this over thirty-plus years in the business, so there is no need to gulp it all down in one bite.

Use this book to gently remind you about how to read copy. Use it as a resource. Please refer back to it again and again. That is how the techniques will become reflexive. I have to apply the same techniques myself over and over.

I have had great sustained success in the voiceover business, and I have worked hard to get and stay there. I have put what I learned in this book so you can prepare ahead of time and not get hit broadside. I wrote this book to get down on paper my techniques that I teach every day so you can avoid the minefields I hit. If you play golf, you know that if you hit the ball in the woods, you adjust and fix it for the next stroke—smooth, straight, and even.

Of course, there will be elation and disappointment. Sometimes you will be perfect and get cast, and other times you will do a great read and not get cast. It's a joyous, erratic, and at times maddening business in terms of how you do or don't get cast. Simply, it starts with the writer having that voice in his or her head, which you can only hope is yours. It continues with you being the easy castable choice from past work and from the writer feeling comfortable with your read and style. That plays into your contacts and your commitment to getting better.

After reading this book, if you decide to either begin or go further, good for you. That commitment means a lot in keeping going in this business. Gain joy from a good audition or from learning a new vocal style. Gain joy from marketing yourself and keeping your name out there in the VO community. Gain joy from setting up a part-time business that could reap you some great results or, at the bare minimum, improve your ability to communicate and work in front of a microphone and to record and edit scripts. And, of course, gain joy from and have gratitude for the great work you will get and how it will lift your life to new heights. It's all good.

Keep trying and never give up. You will have your ups and downs. Get better and meet more people, and great things should happen. Be good to yourself and let yourself make mistakes that will open the door to your greatness.
Stay in touch with me. Check out my website at Ultimatevoiceover.com for teaching tools and programs.

That's it for now. Thanks again for buying this book and learning what it has to offer. Bring it with you to auditions and sessions. Apply and reapply the techniques and tips. Enjoy the voiceover business, get your result and most of all, good luck!!

—Jeff

<u>Testimonials:</u>

> Hi, Jeff! Thanks to you, I landed a steady VO gig doing online commercials. I'm moving to Japan in a few months (only for a year) and I'll be able to work from wherever!
> I just wanted to say thank you thank you thank you for all of your training and advice!
> It was indispensable!
>
> —Paige Saliba
>
> Jeff has a very matter-of-fact, practical approach to this whole acting thing that's devoid of the usual head-in-the-clouds BS

of many acting classes I've taken. I appreciate that perspective. Jeff really pays attention to *your* voice and works with you on developing your own, unique style. I couldn't ask for a better teacher in this field. So...thanks!

—Sam Miller

Taking Jeff's Intermediate Voiceover class at the Acting Studio in Chicago was one of the most educating and exciting experiences for me. Jeff is a fountain of knowledge when it comes to the voiceover industry. You can trust and believe in his direction to bring out the best performance in his students. He is always there to provide guidance and answer any questions you have (while having a wicked sense of humor). Anyone interested in expanding themselves in their craft would greatly benefit from Jeff Lupetin's course. I guarantee it.

—Sheila M. Gagne

Jeff's voiceover class has already improved my skills as a disc jockey and radio announcer. Last night I aired a special program I'd prepared to salute Johnny Otis and Etta James. After I read from a script that I had written, a listener called in to compliment my work, saying that my reading sounded "like poetry." That is a first—and I have Jeff to thank!

—Leslie Keros

I feel like I have learned so much in a very brief time. He is professional, successful and willing to share everything he knows! It was worth every penny to be in the presence of his genius!

—Sariann Monaco

> It's been 4 years since I was in the studio doing my commercial voiceover demo. On that day, Jeff Lupetin and David Leffel recommended that I take improv and acting classes as well. I had only planned on taking one improv class and one acting class, but improv was so much fun and I fell in love with acting. Look at me now. In the past year I have played the role of 13 different characters, not even counting all the characters for my acting classes before that. Never did I think I would be where I am now when I started taking voice over classes. It only gets better with time.
>
> —Richard Esteras

Thanks, guys!